Die drei Pintos

RECENT RESEARCHES IN MUSIC

A-R Editions publishes seven series of critical editions, spanning the history of Western music, American music, and oral traditions.

RECENT RESEARCHES IN THE MUSIC OF THE MIDDLE AGES AND EARLY RENAISSANCE
 Charles M. Atkinson, general editor

RECENT RESEARCHES IN THE MUSIC OF THE RENAISSANCE
 James Haar, general editor

RECENT RESEARCHES IN THE MUSIC OF THE BAROQUE ERA
 Christoph Wolff, general editor

RECENT RESEARCHES IN THE MUSIC OF THE CLASSICAL ERA
 Eugene K. Wolf, general editor

RECENT RESEARCHES IN THE MUSIC OF THE NINETEENTH AND EARLY TWENTIETH CENTURIES
 Rufus Hallmark, general editor

RECENT RESEARCHES IN AMERICAN MUSIC
 John M. Graziano, general editor

RECENT RESEARCHES IN THE ORAL TRADITIONS OF MUSIC
 Philip V. Bohlman, general editor

Each edition in *Recent Researches* is devoted to works by a single composer or to a single genre. The content is chosen for its high quality and historical importance, and each edition includes a substantial introduction and critical report. The music is engraved according to the highest standards of production using the proprietary software MUSE, owned by MusicNotes, Inc.

For information on establishing a standing order to any of our series, or for editorial guidelines on submitting proposals, please contact:

A-R Editions, Inc.
801 Deming Way
Madison, Wisconsin 53717

800 736-0070 (U.S. book orders)
608 836-9000 (phone)
608 831-8200 (fax)
http://www.areditions.com

RECENT RESEARCHES IN THE MUSIC OF THE NINETEENTH AND EARLY TWENTIETH CENTURIES, 30

Gustav Mahler

Die drei Pintos

Based on Sketches and Original Music of
Carl Maria von Weber

Part I:

Introduction, Libretto, Act 1, Entr'act

Edited by James L. Zychowicz

Libretto Translated by
Charlotte Brancaforte and Salvatore Calomino

A-R Editions, Inc.
Madison

A-R Editions, Inc., Madison, Wisconsin 53717
© 2000 by A-R Editions, Inc.

All rights reserved. No part of this book may be reproduced or transmitted in any form by any electronic or mechanical means (including photocopying, recording, or information storage and retrieval) without permission in writing from the publisher.

The purchase of this edition does not convey the right to perform it in public, nor to make a recording of it for any purpose. Such permission must be obtained in advance from the publisher.

A-R Editions is pleased to support scholars and performers in their use of *Recent Researches* material for study or performance. Subscribers to any of the *Recent Researches* series, as well as patrons of subscribing institutions, are invited to apply for information about our "Copyright Sharing Policy."

Printed in the United States of America

ISBN 0-89579-423-3
ISSN 0193-5364

∞ The paper used in this publication meets the minimum requirements of the American National Standard for Information Sciences—Permanence of Paper for Printed Library Materials, ANSI Z39.48-1984.

Contents

Part I

Acknowledgments   vii

Introduction   ix

   Weber and *Die drei Pintos*   ix
   Die drei Pintos after Weber's Death   x
   Mahler and *Die drei Pintos*   xi
   The Completion and Premiere of *Die drei Pintos*   xv
   Die drei Pintos and the Problem of Authorship   xvi
   Performance Considerations   xvii
   Notes   xviii

Libretto and Translation   xxi

   Personen / Characters   xxi
   Ort der Handlung / Scene of the Action   xxii
   Erster Aufzug / Act One   xxii
   Zweiter Aufzug / Act Two   xliii
   Dritter Aufzug / Act Three   lii

Plates   lxxiv

Die drei Pintos

I. Aufzug   3

   No. 1. Ensemble (Gaston, Ambrosio, Chorus): "Leeret die Becher"   3
   No. 2. Rondo a la Polacca (Gaston): "Was ich dann thu'"   47
   No. 3. Terzettino (Gaston, Ambrosio, Der Wirth): "Ei, wer hätte das gedacht!"   59
   No. 4. Romanze von dem verliebten Kater Mansor (Inez): "Leise weht' es"   63
   No. 5. Seguidilla a dos (Inez, Gaston): "Wir, die den Musen dienen"   68
   No. 6. Terzett (Gaston, Ambrosio, Pinto): "Also frisch das Werk begonnen"   85
   No. 7. Finale (Inez, Gaston, Ambrosio, Pinto, Chorus): "Auf das Wohlergeh'n der Gäste!"   134

Entr'act   206

Part II

II. Aufzug   237

   No. 8. Introduction und Ensemble (Clarissa, Laura, Pantaleone, Chorus): "Wißt Ihr nicht, was wir hier sollen?"   237
   No. 9. Ariette (Laura): "'Höchste Lust'"   301
   No. 10. Rezitativ und Arie (Clarissa): "Ach, wenn das Du doch vermöchtest" / "Wonne, süßes Hoffnungsträumen"   305
   No. 11. Duett (Clarissa, Gomez): "Ja, das Wort"   321
   No. 12. Terzett-Finale (Clarissa, Laura, Gomez): "Geschwind nur von hinnen"   336

III. Aufzug   359

   No. 13. Lied mit Chor (Laura, Chorus): "Schmücket die Halle"   359
   No. 14. Duett (Gaston, Ambrosio): "Nun da sind wir"   378
   No. 15. Terzettino (Laura, Gaston, Ambrosio): "Mädchen, ich leide heiße
              Liebespein"   398
   No. 16. Ariette (Ambrosio): "Ein Mädchen verloren"   403
   No. 17. Rondo-Terzett (Gomez, Gaston, Ambrosio): "Ihr, der so edel"   411
   No. 18. Chor (Chorus): "Habt Ihr es denn schon vernommen?"   434
   No. 19. Mädchenlied (Chorus): "Mit lieblichen Blumen"   451
   No. 20. Finale A (Clarissa, Laura, Gomez, Gaston, Ambrosio, Pantaleone,
              Pinto, Chorus): "Was wollt Ihr?"   460
   No. 21. Finale B (Clarissa, Laura, Gomez, Gaston, Ambrosio, Pantaleone, Chorus):
              "Heil sei Euch"   530

Critical Report   561

   Sources   561
   Editorial Methods   561
   Critical Notes   563
   Mahler's Revisions for the Kahnt Score   567
   Text Cues in the Kahnt Score   569
   Notes   570

Acknowledgments

I would like to acknowledge the assistance of a number of individuals toward the completion of this edition. Dr. Charlotte Brancaforte and Dr. Salvatore Calomino, University of Wisconsin, Madison, were extremely generous and gracious with their time in working with me on reading and refining the translation of the libretto. Their sense of style and suggestions of phrasing were essential for the translated text which is part of this edition. Dr. Frank Hirschbach, University of Minnesota, Minneapolis, offered wonderful assistance in deciphering difficult script. Dr. Stephen McClatchie, University of Regina, who worked with the Gustav Mahler-Alfred Rosé Collection of the University of Western Ontario, London, shared with me family letters of Mahler concerning *Die drei Pintos*. M. Henry-Louis de La Grange, of the Bibliothèque musicale Gustav Mahler, Paris, allowed me to consult his copy of the source score. For responses to various inquiries I am indebted to Frau Emmy Hauswirth and Frau Gerda Hanf of the Internationale Gustav Mahler Gesellschaft, Vienna; Dr. Edward R. Reilly, Vassar College; and Geraldine Laudati, Mills Music Library, University of Wisconsin, Madison. I would also like to thank various friends for their interest in this work, including Dr. James Deaville, Dr. Robert Bailey, Steven D. Coburn, Ms. Lynn Ostro, and Mr. Phillip M. Henry. Dr. Salvatore Calomino offered much support and assistance in yet another long-term project. Of course, my mother Mrs. Jean A. Zychowicz and my aunt Ms. Mary Matuszak helped immensely in many ways, for which I remain grateful.

I would like to dedicate this edition to the memory of two people that I know would have appreciated it: to the novelist Robertson Davies, whom I never knew personally, but whose novel *The Lyre of Orpheus* helped me to gain a fresh and different perspective on posthumous collaborations on operas; and to my friend Kenneth Martaus, who died before this edition was finished, but who would have taken delight in the music.

Introduction

Die drei Pintos is an opera that Gustav Mahler (1860–1911) composed from sketches and other music by Carl Maria von Weber (1786–1826). In approaching the materials which Weber left unfinished, Mahler reworked music by the earlier composer to arrive at a finished and performable score. Mahler gave the work its ultimate shape, and the level of intervention required to complete the score went far beyond the conventional role of orchestrator or arranger usually assigned to him for this work. Mahler's efforts brought to the stage the only opera that Weber had not finished in his lifetime.

Weber began his work on the comic opera *Die drei Pintos* in 1820, but by the time of his death, he had sketched only the projected numbers for act 1 and a duet planned for act 2. In the following decades, other composers, notably Giacomo Meyerbeer, attempted to create a performing version of the opera from the sketches, but none succeeded.[1] Yet at the time of Weber's centenary, his grandson Carl von Weber showed the surviving materials to Mahler, who arrived at a way to complete the opera successfully. Mahler himself conducted its premiere in 1888 and the work was generally well received during his lifetime. For various reasons, however, *Die drei Pintos* became lost to subsequent generations, and it currently remains outside the canonical works of both Weber and Mahler. *Die drei Pintos* is nevertheless worthy of consideration on its own merits, since it contains music of both composers and constitutes the only opera project Mahler realized in his career.

The full score prepared for the premiere by professional copyists under the supervision of Mahler was published as a lithograph by C. F. Kahnt; it was not made available for sale to the general public but served as a rental score controlled by the publisher.[2] C. F. Kahnt also published a piano-vocal score of the opera, but Mahler was probably not directly involved with its preparation.[3] Until the present, *Die drei Pintos* has not been available in a modern, critical edition. The abortive collected edition of Weber's works, which commenced in 1926, did not include *Die drei Pintos* among the few volumes it published.[4] At the same time, Mahler's completion of the work will not become part of the *Mahler Gesamtausgabe* nor of the *Supplement* to it.[5] The Internationale Gustav Mahler Gesellschaft has never been explicit about its reasons for excluding *Die drei Pintos*, but the *Gesamtausgabe* so far contains the composer's original compositions and does not extend to music that Mahler arranged or otherwise adapted. The philosophical and philological problems of authorship in the context of Mahler's works are factors that must have influenced decisions about the nature of the *Gesamtausgabe* and the exclusion of *Die drei Pintos*.

For Mahler, however, *Die drei Pintos* was an important work of apprenticeship which occupied him between the cantata *Das klagende Lied* (1880) and the completion of the First Symphony (1888). It was also a key work in his career as a conductor, earning him notice throughout Europe, particularly in German-speaking countries. His score deserves to be known for its realization of Weber's sketches and for its assimilation of Weber's style.

Weber and *Die drei Pintos*

While completing *Der Freischütz* in the spring of 1820, Weber began work on the opera *Die drei Pintos*. The basis for the opera was the novella *Der Brautkampf* by Carl Seidel, with the libretto written by Theodor Hell (Karl Gottfried Theodor Winkler).[6] *Die drei Pintos* was to be lighter in character than *Der Freischütz*. The plot involves three suitors to a bride, all claiming to be the true groom, whom no one in the bride's family had ever seen. Set in Spain, the work allowed for some exotic elements and included several large scenes with the full ensemble of soloists, chorus, and orchestra. Various projects kept Weber from proceeding with his plans, including his work on the music for *Preciosa*. Nevertheless, some of the sketches for *Die drei Pintos* emerged at the same time as *Preciosa*, which was given its premiere in March 1821, and the connections between *Die drei Pintos* and Weber's other music are borne out in the surviving manuscripts. For example, the sketches for a recitative and aria, "Ach wenn dies du doch" / "Wonnigsüsses Hoffnungsträumen" (see table 1, no. 2), are found on the page that contains a draft for Weber's *Konzertstück* for piano and orchestra; and the sketches for a duet, "Ja, sie wird," and a trio, "Geschwind nur von hinnen" (table 1, nos. 3a and 3b), occur on the same leaf as a draft of the finale to the second act of *Der Freischütz*.[7]

Regarding the work he did accomplish on *Die drei Pintos*, Weber went so far as to indicate the keys, many meters, and some approximate durations of the seventeen planned numbers (the overture and sixteen numbered

TABLE 1
Weber's Plan for *Die drei Pintos*

Act	Number	Hell's Description	Weber's Sketches
		Overture: D major; 2/4	None
1	1	Introduction: B-flat major; 4/4, 3/4, 6/8; 9 minutes	Introduction: Chorus with Clarissa, Laura, and Pantaleone, "Wisst ihr nicht"
	2	Aria (Clarissa): D major; **C**, 3/4; 7½ minutes (± 1½)	Recitative and Aria: Clarissa, "Ach wenn dies du doch" / "Wonnnigsüsses Hoffnungsträumen"
	3	Duett and Terzett: E-flat major; 4/4, 3/4; 9 minutes (± 2)	3a, Duett: Clarissa and Gomez, "Ja, sie wird"
			3b, Terzett: Clarissa, Gomez, and Laura, "Geschwind nur von hinnen"
	4	Canzonetta (Gaston and Inez): C major; 3/4; 5 minutes	Duett, Seguidillos à dos: Inez and Gaston, "Wir den Musen"
	5	Terzetto: B major; 9 minutes (± 3)	Terzett: Gaston, Pinto, and Ambrosio, "Also frisch"
	6	Finale: D major; 4/4, 6/8; 9 minutes	Finale: Inez, Gaston, Pinto, and Chorus, "Auf das Wohlsinn"
2	7	Duetto: G major; 2/4	Duett: Gaston and Ambrosio, "Nun da sind wir"
	8	Aria (Gomez): C major	None
	9	Duett: A major	None
	10	Aria (Pinto): E major; 2/4	None
	11	with Chorus: E-flat major	None
	12	Finale: F major; 3/4; 5–6 [minutes]	None
3	13	Quintetto: E major	None
	14	Aria (Pantaleone): C major	None
	15	Romanze: A-flat major	None
	16	Finale: D major	None

pieces, as shown in table 1). The sketches contain ideas for only seven of the numbers, some of which are single-line fragments while others are more extensive. Of the latter, several pages are in short score, and the opening of the introduction to the opera occurs in a full-score draft. While the music is in the early stages of composition, several numbers contain passages that are crossed out, with insertions sometimes occurring at various places on the page. Weber also set some of the text, but it was hastily written, as though it were meant as a reminder for the composer himself.

As such, Weber's sketches are intelligible in the context of Hell's libretto, which, despite several divergences from Seidel's *Der Brautkampf*, is closer to the plot of the novella than is the revised libretto that Mahler eventually set.[8] It is difficult to assess fully the merits of Hell's libretto since Weber did not complete his setting of it and may have revised its organization had he finished it.[9] John Warrack refers to Weber's sporadic work on *Die drei Pintos* throughout 1821,[10] but with the formal refusal to produce the opera in Dresden, Weber set it aside and began to explore the possibilities of composing other music for the stage. When Domenico Barbaia asked Weber for an opera for the 1822–23 season at the Kärntnertor Theater in Vienna, however, he considered either returning to *Die drei Pintos* or taking up work on *Euryanthe*.[11] Even though he chose to do the latter,[12] Weber worked on *Die drei Pintos* as late as 1824,[13] but in the end he sketched only seven numbers, with all but one for the first act.[14]

Die drei Pintos after Weber's Death

After the composer's death, the prospect of an unperformed opera by Weber emerged with the suggestion that something more than fragmentary sketches actually existed. Weber's plans to compose *Die drei Pintos* were known to several of his intimates, including his biographer Julius Benedict, who attested to having heard the entirety of the first act from the composer himself.[15] No score for the entire opera or even a complete act ever emerged. The surviving sketches, which F. W. Jähns collated and copied, eventually became part of the collection of *Weberiana*.[16] Nevertheless, rumors persisted that Weber had indeed completed the opera and that a score existed.[17]

Weber's widow Caroline intended to have the music found in the sketches brought to performance in some format, and she worked to have *Die drei Pintos* completed during the quarter century after Weber's death. While some musicians who looked at the sketches, such as Heinrich Esser (1818–72), Ludwig Spohr (1784–1859), and Karol Józef Lipiński (1790–1861), judged them to be unworkable, even undecipherable,[18] Caroline von Weber believed the situation to be otherwise. Karl Gottlieb Reissiger (1798–1859), who succeeded Weber as conductor in Dresden, expressed an interest in working on the opera and even produced an arrangement of one sketched number,[19] but Caroline asked Giacomo Meyerbeer (1791–1864) to complete *Die drei Pintos*. Since

Meyerbeer had known Weber and both composers had studied with Abbé (Georg Joseph) Vogler (1749–1814), Meyerbeer seemed to be a natural choice for the project.

Although Meyerbeer attempted to finish *Die drei Pintos* and returned to the sketches time and again, he ultimately failed to produce an opera based on the subject. While it has been suggested that Meyerbeer simply held onto the sketches for approximately twenty years without working on them,[20] the evidence of Meyerbeer's diaries and letters demonstrates, on the contrary, his continual efforts to work on the opera and also his recurrent frustration with arriving at what he believed would be a suitable libretto for the work.[21] He determined that to complete *Die drei Pintos* one would have to draw on other music of Weber—as Mahler himself later did. After various attempts to work on the opera, including the idea of a version entitled "Die beiden Pintos" (1845), Meyerbeer decided to return the sketches for *Die drei Pintos* to the Weber family in 1852.[22]

While Vinzenz Lachner (1811–93)[23] at one time expressed his interest in working on *Die drei Pintos,* nothing came of it. After the death of Caroline von Weber, the materials for the opera went to Weber's son Max Maria von Weber, and when he died in 1881 the sketches were passed on to his own son, Captain Carl von Weber, who then lived in Leipzig. Weber's grandson Carl seemed to have a personal interest in the sketches, which was borne out by his work with Mahler on completing the opera.

Mahler and *Die drei Pintos*

It is useful to view Mahler's decision to work on *Die drei Pintos* in light of his attempts to compose operas from early in his career. Although his initial opera projects, *Die Argonauten* and *Herzog Ernst von Schwaben,* fell by the wayside, and despite his growing interest in composing symphonic music after he collaborated with Rudolf Krzyzanowski (1859–1911) on the piano reduction of Bruckner's Third Symphony, his first major work, the cantata *Das klagende Lied* (1880), was dramatic in nature. He subsequently wrote the libretto for the projected opera *Rübezahl* (1883), for which no music survives. Yet the impulse to compose an opera ultimately emerged in the work on *Die drei Pintos* that Mahler undertook in 1887.

The circumstances that led Mahler to take on this project stemmed from his associations in Leipzig, where he served as conductor under Arthur Nikisch at the Neues Stadttheater.[24] Mahler worked with Nikisch on conducting a cycle of Weber's operas to celebrate the composer's centenary,[25] and this brought him closer to work on the unfinished opera. In May 1887 Mahler met Carl von Weber through Max Staegemann, who was then director at the Neues Stadttheater. It must have been soon after this meeting that Mahler studied the sketches and discovered the problem that others before him had already encountered, namely, the relative paucity of material that Weber had actually left. At one point, Mahler intended to present the sketches in an edition along with his own version of the opera, but Staegemann and Carl von Weber were able to convince him to proceed with a completion of *Die drei Pintos* for performance in Leipzig.

An important factor in Mahler's decision to pursue a completion of the opera lay in the revised libretto that Carl von Weber prepared. Hell's text was an obstacle for Meyerbeer, and it is not clear whether Mahler also began work with Hell's libretto or turned immediately to Carl von Weber's revision. It is possible that Mahler referred to Hell's text as he worked out some of the ideas in the sketched numbers and only later, when he agreed to proceed with *Die drei Pintos* as a three-act opera, used the text of Carl von Weber. While the plot remains essentially the same from Seidel's novella,[26] to Hell's libretto, to the final libretto based on Carl von Weber's revision with changes introduced by Mahler in the course of composition (see table 2), the structure of the final libretto departs in significant ways from the libretto by Hell that Weber intended to use. The principal differences include a new opening number (which allowed for a large set-piece with soloists and chorus), the addition of scenes for Clarissa, Laura, and Gomez as Don Pantaleone announces the marriage plans and they prepare for the arrival of Don Pinto (which accounts for the whole of act 2, nos. 8 through 12), and in general, more emphasis on the roles of Don Gaston and his servant Ambrosio. The latter two appear in the new opening scene, which helps to unite the beginning of the opera with its close.

Having an acceptable three-act plan before him, Mahler was in a position to address the problem of how to complete the opera, given the few sketches Weber had left. First, he redistributed the original sketched numbers to each of the three acts rather than leaving them all at the beginning (compare tables 1 and 3). He then reworked unpublished music by Weber for the remaining numbers. In this way Mahler avoided a score with the first act containing all of Weber's sketches and the other two becoming essentially a pastiche.

Mahler's own testimony about the work that he did on the opera focused mainly on the process of deciphering and realizing the sketches. According to Natalie Bauer-Lechner:

> [Carl von] Weber had told him about his grandfather's sketches, which he had already shown to many capable musicians, without finding anyone who dared think it possible to salvage anything from those rough hints—let alone transform them into a whole. He begged Mahler to take the sketches home with him and see if he could succeed in raising the sunken treasure.
>
> For days on end, Mahler had the sketches lying on his piano, immersing himself in them. But he could not break the spell that bound them. Then—it was on a brilliant afternoon, and Weber's pages were streaked with coloured shafts of sunlight—the complete structure of one number came to him. He ran straight to the Webers and played it to them, to their great delight. From that moment on, one number after another came to him until in about a week all of the material had been worked out and completed. Having set about the work in the most faithful and conscientious fashion, respecting every note of Weber's and developing it in the way it seemed to suggest, Mahler would

TABLE 2
The Evolution of the Libretto for *Die drei Pintos*

Seidel (novella)	Hell (libretto)	Weber/Mahler (libretto)	Comments
		At an inn, Don Gaston Viratos takes his leave from the students at Salamanca.	Weber/Mahler libretto casts new emphasis on Don Gaston and Ambrosio.
		Gaston complains to Ambrosio of his loveless state and then discovers how much money he spent at the inn.	
		Ambrosio meets the innkeeper's daughter Inez, who is hardly sympathetic to him and Gaston.	Note early introduction of Inez.
Part I. Don Pantaleone de Pacheco decides that his daughter Clarissa will marry Don Nunno de Fonseca, who did a service for Pantaleone years earlier	Don Pantaleone de Pacheco has given his niece Clarissa to be married to Don Pinto de Fonseca, but neither Clarissa nor her maid Laura know him.		Laura becomes Clarissa's maid, not Gomez's sister as in the novella.
Pantaleone contacts Nunno but because Nunno is very old, he suggests his son Don Pinto marry Clarissa.			The elder Fonseca, Don Nunno, does not appear in the last version of the libretto.
Clarissa is in love with Don Gomez Freires.			
Don Gaston Viratos and his servant Ambrosio encounter Pinto at an inn and discover his plan to marry Clarissa.	The student Don Gaston and his servant Ambrosio meet Pinto, and upon hearing his story, decide to take his place.	Don Pinto arrives, and upon hearing his tale, Gaston decides to prevent him from going further with his plan to marry Clarissa.	
When Pinto becomes drunk and collapses, Gaston assumes his identity.	With the help of the innkeeper's daughter Inez, Gaston, and Ambrosio proceed with their plot.	Gaston gets Pinto drunk and leaves for Pantaleone's house with the papers that identify him as Pinto.	Note the introduction and identity of the innkeeper's daughter Inez in Hell's libretto.
		At their home, Clarissa and her maid Laura are told of Pantaleone's plans to have her marry Pinto, but she is in love with Don Gomez.	
		Laura seeks out Gomez and brings him to Clarissa. The three determine to find a way out of the situation.	
A servant offers to take Gaston/Pinto to Pantaleone.			

TABLE 2 (CONTINUED)

Seidel (novella)	Hell (libretto)	Weber/Mahler (libretto)	Comments
Part II. Gaston/Pinto finds himself at the home of Gomez.	En route to Clarissa, Gaston meets Don Gomez, who takes him for the real Pinto.	After the women finish decorating the hall for a feast, Gaston and Ambrosio arrive at Pantaleone's and meet Laura, who takes Gaston for Pinto.	
Gomez asks Gaston/Pinto not to marry a woman he does not love or else fight to the death.		Gomez encounters Gaston and demands that Gaston give up his suit.	
Gomez offers the hand of his sister Laura to Gaston, who offers to assist Gomez in winning Clarissa.	Gaston offers to help Gomez win Clarissa by giving him the papers he took from Pinto.	Gaston offers to assist Gomez in his suit of Clarissa by suggesting that Gomez become Pinto.	
As Pinto, Gomez arrives at the celebration Pantaleone has in his honor, and Clarissa is amazed.	Gaston and Gomez arrive at the home of Pantaleone and are welcomed there.	As Gaston arrives with Gomez, and Gomez is welcomed as Pinto,	
Part III. The elder Fonseca arrives to meet his son and discovers the deception.			
Gomez reveals the ruse and assures the elder Fonseca that Pinto will soon arrive.			
Part IV. Pinto arrives and the elder Fonseca demands that his son fight for his bride.	Pinto arrives and Gaston declares him to be an imposter.	Pinto suddenly arrives and confusion ensues.	
	At the feast to celebrate the betrothal, Don Nunno de Fonseca arrives, and Pinto is found to be genuine.		
When Gomez first strikes Pinto, Pinto gives up the fight and surrenders his interest in Clarissa.		Gaston challenges Pinto, and Pinto responds in a cowardly way.	
Gaston intervenes and Gomez is offered Clarissa's hand, since Pantaleone finds the Fonsecas a disgrace.		Pantaleone finds Pinto a disgrace but admires now the perseverance of Gomez.	
Gaston marries Laura; Gomez marries Clarissa and Ambrosio marries her maid; Pinto marries the daughter of an innkeeper.	After some confusion about the identities, Gomez is allowed to marry Clarissa, and the opera ends.	Pantaleone allows Gomez and Clarissa to marry.	The fate of Pinto is not explicitly stated in the opera librettos.

TABLE 3
The Completed Numbers and their Sources in Mahler's Version of *Die drei Pintos*

Act	Number	Title	Pages in Kahnt Score	Source (by Weber, unless indicated otherwise)
1	1	Ensemble, "Leeret die Becher"	3–24	"Das Turnierbankett," op. 68
	2	Rondo a la Polacca, "Was ich dann thu'"	25–33	Weber's "Insertion" for Haydn's opera *Der Freybrief*
	3	Terzettino, "Ei, wer hätte das gedacht!"	33–35	Three-part folksong from "Volkslieder, mit neuen Weisen versehen"
	4	Romanze von dem verliebten Kater Mansor, "Leise weht' es"	36–39	"Romanze von Alkazor und Zaide" from Weber's "Insertion" to Kind's *Das Nachtlager von Granada*
	5	Seguidilla a dos, "Wir, die den Musen dienen"	40–49	*Pintos*, sketch no. 4
	6	Terzett, "Also frisch das Werk begonnen"	50–79	*Pintos*, sketch no. 5
	7	Finale, "Auf das Wohlergeh'n der Gäste!"	80–124	*Pintos*, sketch no. 6
		Entr'act	1–16	Original composition by Mahler based on themes by Weber
2	8	Introduction und Ensemble, "Wißt Ihr nicht, was wir hier sollen?"	1–39	*Pintos*, sketch no. 1
	9	Ariette, "'Höchste Lust'"	40–43	"Triolett" from "Gesänge und Lieder," op. 71; "Waltz" from "Ariette für Lucinda" for Kauer's *Das Sternenmädchen*
	10	Rezitativ und Arie, "Ach, wenn das Du doch vermöchtest" / "Wonne, süßes Hoffnungsträumen"	44–54	*Pintos*, sketch no. 2
	11	Duett, "Ja, das Wort"	55–63	*Pintos*, sketch no. 3a
	12	Terzett-Finale, "Geschwind nur von hinnen"	64–78	*Pintos*, sketch no. 3b
3	13	Lied mit Chor, "Schmücket die Halle"	1–11	"Festchor," no. 7 from *Jubelkantate*
	14	Duett, "Nun da sind wir"	12–23	*Pintos*, sketch no. 7
	15	Terzettino, "Mädchen, ich leide heiße Liebespein"	24–27	"Three-part canon" from "Fünf Gesänge mit Gittarenbegleitung," op. 13
	16	Ariette, "Ein Mädchen verloren"	28–33	Aria, "Mein Weib ist kapores," Weber's insertion to Fischer's *Der travestirte Aeneas*
	17	Rondo-Terzett, "Ihr, der so edel"	34–49	"Romanze ("Elle était simple et gentilette") für Gesang und Klavier"; Weber's "Gesang der Nurmahal" for Moore's *Lalla Rookh*
	18	Chor, "Habt Ihr es denn schon vernommen?"	50–59	*Pintos*, sketch no. 1
	19	Mädchenlied, "Mit lieblichen Blumen"	60–64	"Chorus," no. 4 from *Den Sachsen-Sohn*
	20	Finale A, "Was wollt Ihr?"	65–115	Original composition by Mahler based on themes (from act 1) by Weber
	21	Finale B, "Heil sei Euch"	116–35	*Pintos*, sketch no. 7

have much preferred to publish his completed version together with the original sketches (which are in Weber's possession) and then have it performed as such. But Weber and [Max] Stägemann (the director of the Leipzig Opera) were united in their insistence that it should be turned into a full-scale opera. Weber wanted to write the text, and Mahler was to add the necessary music. So that is how the *Pintos* came into being.

"You'd be surprised," said Mahler, "to see how little was actually composed by Weber: not much more than a few wonderful themes, not a note of orchestration. So I had to write by far the greater part of the work. And, hesitant as I was at first in completing the sketches, I grew all the bolder as the work progressed. I let myself be carried away by the subject and by my own inspiration, and forgot to worry about whether Weber would have done it that way. In the end, I simply let myself go and composed as I felt inclined; I became more and more 'Mahlerish,' until finally, when I drafted and worked out the new section, every single note was my own. (Even in the text, I did a lot without asking my librettist or signing my name to it.) And it is precisely these new numbers which were most highly praised by critics and public afterwards, and which were considered 'pure Weber.'"[27]

The process of choosing and adapting unpublished works of Weber was complicated, and Mahler probably expended as much effort reworking them as it would have taken him to compose entirely new pieces for the opera. The unpublished works Mahler drew upon are enumerated by Warrack in his study and are listed in table 3 opposite the numbers that are based on them.[28] Mahler is nowhere explicit about his criteria for making selections, and it may be that he chose some pieces at the suggestion of Carl von Weber or his wife Marion.[29] It does appear, however, that Mahler was careful to select pieces that incorporated the voice rather than attempt to add voices to instrumental works. In any case, his decision to exclude published music, and especially any music from Weber's completed operas, helped insure that the music used in *Die drei Pintos* would not carry associations from other known works.

For the most part, Weber's music was only the starting point for larger and more complex structures, as with the transformation of the chorus from the *Jubelkantate* into the opening number in act 3 (no. 13). Similarly, to create the third-act trio (no. 17) Mahler used two songs Weber had composed for different purposes and gave them a new context in *Die drei Pintos*. By manipulating Weber's own music throughout the opera, Mahler was able to complete the work in the style of the earlier composer. This extends to the two numbers generally regarded as Mahler's own, the entr'act[30] and the first part of the finale in act 3 (no. 20), both of which are firmly based on themes of Weber, rather than music Mahler composed anew for the opera.

By relying on less well-known music of Weber, rather than numbers from Weber's completed operas, Mahler avoided making *Die drei Pintos* into a pastiche. This approach avoided introducing into his score associations that would distract from the new work. More impor-

tantly, Mahler chose music which fit the musical structure of his score. He did not take a chorus of Weber and rework it in his score as an aria, nor otherwise alter the texture of his source material. While by the standards of the late twentieth century some of Mahler's choices may seem arbitrary, the approach he took in completing the opera is internally consistent.

Moreover, the assemblage of sketch material and unpublished music of Weber results in a chrestomathy, that is, a collection of Weber's own music, which lends an air of authenticity to Mahler's score. Yet the effort it took to make the various ideas function within the structure of an opera goes beyond the concept of chrestomathy or pastiche. It is certainly much more than an arrangement, as some would have it. In manipulating Weber's music into a convincing score, Mahler exceeded the expectations others may have had for the completer of *Die drei Pintos*.[31] The result is a score that is unique as the product of two strong musical personalities.

The Completion and Premiere of *Die drei Pintos*

While Mahler disclosed some of the details of his efforts on *Die drei Pintos* to Bauer-Lechner in October 1901, little material exists from the time when he actually worked on it. The published letters contain few references to the opera, but the family letters[32] include more information. The gist of this material reveals little more about its genesis than Mahler confided to Bauer-Lechner over a decade later. Nevertheless, these letters convey the tenacity and exuberance of the young composer on the brink of completing a new work, and in them, Mahler writes about *Die drei Pintos* as though the opera were his very own.

One of the earliest references to *Die drei Pintos* in Mahler's correspondence occurs on 7 September 1887,[33] when he told his parents about his playing part of the work for Staegemann and others at the Opera. A month later on 4 October 1887,[34] he reported that the score was completed and in the hands of the copyist, and that the premiere was to be in December. The remarks in the following month[35] concerning the second act suggest work on the details of the copyist's score. Rehearsals for *Die drei Pintos* began in late November, and at some point the date of the premiere was changed to January.

By the end of November Mahler had worked out the financial arrangements for the publication of the piano-vocal score, as he related some of the details to his parents in a letter from that time.[36] Despite the plans for the score to appear in January 1888, Mahler had rewritten the entr'act in late December 1887.[37] He was obviously immersed in the details of the premiere on 20 January 1888, which was a success. Mahler wrote his parents about it the day after (21 January)[38] and included specific references to music in the opera (his two favorite numbers were the opening student chorus [no. 1] and what he called the "Ballade von Kater Mansor" [no. 4]). He also mentioned his contact with the conductor Hermann Levi from Bayreuth, an important event in Mahler's life, as the premiere of *Die drei Pintos* brought him his first international recognition as composer and conductor.

In the course of his account of Mahler's work on *Die drei Pintos*,[39] La Grange reports the reaction of the press to the opera, and while it is useful to note the enthusiasm at the premiere, not all the responses to the work were uniformly positive. As much as Eduard Hanslick was careful to praise the craft of Mahler's score,[40] he found it necessary to point out that the opera was not so much by Weber but from Weber,[41] that it could never be completed exactly as the composer might have finished it. Richard Strauss was initially delighted with *Die drei Pintos*, that is, until he communicated his thoughts to Hans von Bülow, whereupon what he had at first spoken of as a masterpiece became mediocre and tedious. Strauss's about-face on the opera is revealing for its pedantic criticism of a score he had previously recommended.[42] As for Bülow, he regarded Mahler's completion with disdain: "Wo Weberei, wo Mahlerei—einerlei—das Ganze ist *per Bacco* ein infamer, antiquierter Schmarren" [Here Weber-ly (woven), there Mahler-ly (painted), all the same: the entirety is, by God, a shameless, antiquated mess] (my translation).[43]

From his own subsequent references to his work on the opera, though, Mahler seems to have taken some pride in *Die drei Pintos*. Years later, when he responded in November 1896 to a request for biographical information, he told the critic Richard Batka that "my first public appearance as a creative artist was with the completion of Weber's *Die drei Pintos*."[44] A month later he told the Viennese critic Max Marschalk about his musical coming-of-age with the composition of *Das klagende Lied*, but went on to comment on the place of *Die drei Pintos* in his life:

> [I] faced the public for the first time as completer and arranger of Weber's *Pinto* sketches. I regard that work as far from obsolete and am convinced that it will be taken up again when this clamour for Realism has died down.[45]

When Mahler spoke with Bauer-Lechner several years later, he continued to be satisfied with *Die drei Pintos*.[46] From his standpoint, the opera became more his composition than Weber's, despite having its origin with Weber. The musicologist Guido Adler certainly recognized Mahler's achievement in his account of the composer's life.[47] For Adler, Mahler succeeded not only in completing the work but in capturing the style of Weber even in his own original contributions to the score.

Mahler went on to treat the finished score as though it were one of his own. Just as he would later revise his own works to accommodate second thoughts and further ideas, Mahler returned to *Die drei Pintos* with the intention of improving it. He told Bauer-Lechner about this, and her account shows his capacity for self-criticism:

> Mahler says that his scoring of the *Pintos* is rather clumsy, as he lacked experience and skill at the time. Later when he conducted the work in Prague, he toned down the orchestration considerably. He wrote down the modifications and alterations that he made at that time and sent them to the publisher with the request that they should be added as an appendix to the whole edition. But this was never done, and Mahler did not even receive back his manuscript, which he had sent away without making a copy.[48]

The list of alterations survives and has been reproduced in the critical report below. All the changes have been incorporated into the score for the first time in the present edition.

Die drei Pintos and the Problem of Authorship

Mahler's score for *Die drei Pintos* has historically failed to hold an established place among the works of either Weber or Mahler because of the difficulties that exist regarding its authorship. Considered with Weber's music, *Die drei Pintos* was left incomplete and may have been abandoned. It is impossible to realize the opera exactly as Weber would have composed it, and the sketches do not constitute a score that can be taken into performance without drastic intervention. While *Die drei Pintos* clearly exists as a compositional impulse on Weber's part, it cannot be construed as a "work" as that term is currently understood or as the work-concept became known in the nineteenth century.[49]

The motivation for completing *Die drei Pintos* after Weber's death sprung from his widow Caroline, who may have misjudged the state of the materials. Her idea of finding a composer with a similar background as Weber had its merits. Yet the longer it took a composer of Weber's generation to take on this project, the less likely it seemed that anyone who attempted to complete *Die drei Pintos* could do so convincingly. By the time that Mahler worked on the opera, the fact that he could somehow capture Weber's style seems to have been a novelty that would not have been noticed earlier in the century.

Furthermore, Mahler's score for *Die drei Pintos* extended the gestation of the work over half a century to 1888. By then the sketches lost their original function of jogging the memory of the composer about the way he wanted to proceed. Weber's sketches and other unpublished compositions became materials which Mahler decided to construct into the opera as he envisioned it. In completing the score Mahler arrived at a work which was original with him, although the elements he used for it were Weber's. *Die drei Pintos* became a musical work through Mahler's efforts, which extend traditional understanding of authorship and the role of multiple composers for a single work.

When it comes to accepting *Die drei Pintos* among the works of Mahler, the traditional concept of a musical work hindered its automatic inclusion. When the opera is mentioned in some of the earliest criticism of Mahler, for example, it occurs in discussions of Mahler's work as a conductor, not as a composer,[50] and subsequent references to the score for *Die drei Pintos* in the literature on Mahler occur in discussions of his arrangements.[51]

To identify *Die drei Pintos* as an arrangement can be misleading since, in the strictest sense, an arrangement refers to the reworking of an already completed work.[52] When it comes to Mahler's music, the term arrangement usually applies to his revisions of other composers' music, in the sense of versions he performed at various times in his career and also those editions he published. Mahler's "retouchings" of operas include new editions of Mozart's *Die Hochzeit des Figaros* (for which he contributed an entirely new scene) and Weber's *Euryanthe* and *Oberon* (the latter involved actual rearrangements of several numbers). Yet these revisions do not compare with the kind of work Mahler pursued in creating the score for *Die drei Pintos*, in which he fashioned Weber's sketches and music into the opera and essentially functioned as its composer. It is not so much a matter of determining what is Weber's in this version than it is to understand the integrity Mahler attempted to bring to the score in his manipulation of musical materials. In this sense *Die drei Pintos* in this version is hardly authentic in the purest sense, but it possesses integrity as a work of Mahler.

As to the place of *Die drei Pintos* in the music of either Mahler or Weber, it is impossible to resolve the matter to an absolute degree. It is important to note, however, that soon after Mahler completed the score for the opera, it was included by some among the earlier composer's works. However, Mahler's score became increasingly estranged from the music of Weber. In some ways, this reflects the shift in attitude of the public to the two composers. When Weber was more widely performed in the repertoire, it was possible to include *Die drei Pintos* among his works, since his reputation seems to have been strong enough then to absorb such an ascription. Yet as Mahler's position in the repertoire shifted, his ascendancy could assimilate the inclusion of *Die drei Pintos* among his "arrangements," if not with his own compositions. In succeeding generations the position of *Die drei Pintos* may change again, as the work is rediscovered by new listeners, who know and appreciate equally well the music of Weber and of Mahler.

Performance Considerations

Die drei Pintos has little performance history past Mahler's lifetime, and so lacks the kind of performing tradition that exists for other operas. The work has been performed on occasion, such as for the 1989 Mahler Cycle at Châtelet, Paris, which included a concert presentation of *Die drei Pintos*.[53] This performance was an isolated event and was not tied to a new production or revival of the opera meant to return it to the stage on a regular basis.

The Kahnt rental score upon which this edition is based was prepared under the supervision of Mahler and was used by him in his performances of the opera. It was on the basis of those performances that he sent revisions to the publisher, which he mentioned to Bauer-Lechner (see note 48), asking that they be incorporated into the score or be placed in an appendix. Though the revisions were not published during his lifetime, they established the final state[54] in which he left *Die drei Pintos*. As has been mentioned, the revisions are incorporated and listed (in the critical report) in this edition.

Mahler indicated several possible cuts in the Kahnt score and made several more suggestions for cuts in his later list of revisions. These possible cuts are summarized in table 4 and should be considered as options the conductor may wish to pursue in mounting the work on stage. The cuts should by no means suggest that Mahler wished to alter the structure of the numbers for which they exist; they were meant to shorten the content without affecting the dramaturgy or drastically changing the musical structure. Any other cuts should be avoided, and should the conductor wish to drop a number, it would be at the expense of the opera as a whole.

It is also important to note that the last two numbers of act 3, Finale A and Finale B (nos. 20 and 21), are not optional endings but are two parts of one extended finale. While one commentator has referred to these numbers as "two alternate finales,"[55] a performance using only one of them would make no sense since the plot

TABLE 4
Die drei Pintos: Cuts in Mahler's Score

Number	Mahler's Cut	Source
5	mm. 26–28 (inclusive)	Mahler's list of revisions
6	mm. 118–40 (inclusive)	Kahnt score
	m. 206 (second half) to m. 241 (first half)	Mahler's list of revisions
8	mm. 48–65 (inclusive)	Mahler's list of revisions
	mm. 183–201 (inclusive)	Kahnt score
	mm. 210–16 (inclusive)	Kahnt score
	m. 330 (all) to m. 339 (first beat)	Mahler's list of revisions
10	mm. 120–42 (inclusive)	Kahnt score
14	mm. 1–4 (inclusive)	Mahler's list of revisions
21	mm. 1–47 (inclusive)	Mahler's list of revisions

progresses from one to the other and only concludes with Finale B. The division of the finale into two parts has its origin in the separate origins of the numbers themselves: they are the result of two different compositional processes, with Finale A being an entirely new work composed by Mahler (based on ideas from act 1) and Finale B being a realization of sketches left by Weber. With his decision to present the finale in two parts, Mahler showed his hand, so to speak, by keeping a number he added separate from a number based on sketches.

As always, tempos and dynamics should be adjusted to suit the acoustics of the hall and the ensemble for any given number. Mahler was more detailed in his indication of dynamics for the instruments than for the voices, such that editorial markings have been added where appropriate. Of course, the dynamics of the instruments must always be held relative to what the voices can project so as to insure a clear presentation of the text.

No recordings of any excerpts of the opera exist from Mahler's time. In fact, no recording exists before the one conducted in 1977 by Gary Bertini,[56] which contains all the music for the opera with the dialogue abridged. Yet the juxtaposition of music and dialogue in the "Kater Mansor" scene would be useful to hear, as would other spoken lines serving as lead-ins. Bertini retained enough of the dialogue to suggest the drama in various scenes, but his choices are by no means definitive.

Notes

1. Among those who looked at the sketches were Johannes Brahms (1833–97), who saw them when Max von Weber lived in Vienna (see Richard Heuberger, *Erinnerungen an Johannes Brahms: Tagebuchnotizen aus den Jahren 1875 bis 1897 erstmals vollständig herausgegeben von Kurt Hofmann* [Tutzing: Hans Schneider, 1976], 37), and Eduard Hanslick (1825–1904), as he states in his review of the opera, "Die drei Pintos," in *Musikalisches und Litterarisches*, vol. 5, *Die moderne Oper* (Berlin: Allgemeiner Verein für deutsche Litteratur, 1889), 87–95.

2. Carl Maria von Weber, *Die drei Pintos: Komische Oper in drei Aufzügen*, der dramatische Theil von Carl von Weber, der musikalische Theil von Gustav Mahler (Leipzig: C. F. Kahnt, [1888]), ed. no. 2953.

3. C. M. von Weber, *Die drei Pintos: Komische Oper in drei Aufzügen*, der dramatische Theil von C. von Weber, der musikalische von G. Mahler, Klavier-Auszug mit Text (Leipzig: C. F. Kahnt, [1888]), ed. no. 1455.

4. H. J. Moser, ed., *C. M. von Weber: Musikalische Werke, erste kritische Gesamtausgabe*. The only editions to appear are in the series "Dramatische Werke" (Reihe 2): vol. 1, Jugendopern: *Das stumme Waldmädchen* (*Bruchstücke*) and *Peter Schmoll und seine Nachbarn*, ed. A. Lorenz (Augsburg, 1926); vol. 2, *Rübezahl and Silvana*, ed. W. Kaehler (Augsburg, 1928); and vol. 3, *Preciosa*, ed. L. K. Mayer (Brunswick, 1939). However, the new *Gesamtausgabe* of the composer's works (1997–) will include a version of Weber's sketches for *Die drei Pintos* edited by James L. Zychowicz. This edition will include all the sketches in a diplomatic transcription along with Theodor Hell's libretto. Mahler's completion with the libretto on which he and Carl von Weber collaborated will not be part of this edition.

5. The Mahler *Gesamtausgabe*, published by the Internationale Gustav Mahler Gesellschaft, consists of his collected works in the so-called *Ausgabe letzter Hand* in the Roman-numbered sequence, with variant versions of the music in the Arabic-numbered supplement.

6. As Theodor Hell, Winkler wrote the German translation of J. R. Planché's libretto for Weber's *Oberon*. See *The New Grove Dictionary of Music and Musicians*, s.v. "Winkler, Carl Gottfried Theodor," by Walter Hüttel.

7. Michael C. Tusa, *Euryanthe and Carl Maria von Weber's Dramaturgy of German Opera*, Studies in Musical Genesis and Structure (Oxford: Oxford University Press, 1991), 143–44. Tusa points out that the extant materials for *Euryanthe* also occur with sketches for other music, including *Oberon* and the Bassoon Concerto (pp. 144–45). My table 1 is based on information found in John Warrack, *Carl Maria von Weber*, 2nd ed. (Cambridge: Cambridge University Press, 1976), 258–61, and Friedrich Wilhelm Jähns, *Carl Maria von Weber in seinen Werken: Chronologisch-thematisches Verzeichniss seiner sämtlichen Compositionen* (Berlin: Schlesinger'schen Buch- und Musikhandlung, 1871; reprint, Berlin-Lichterfelde: Robert Lienau, 1967), 417–27.

8. On the relationship of the novella to the opera, see Warrack, *Carl Maria von Weber*, 256–57. See also Jähns, *Carl Maria von Weber in seinen Werken*, 422.

9. As a point of comparison, it is useful to bear in mind the evolution of the libretto for Weber's *Euryanthe* as discussed in Tusa, Euryanthe, 114–40.

10. Warrack, *Carl Maria von Weber*, 240–44.

11. Tusa refers to Weber's decision to pursue work on *Euryanthe* in Euryanthe, 10–12. In his discussion of other works that Weber considered taking up at the time, Tusa's suggestion about an opera on the Spanish hero El Cid (p. 12) echoes the Spanish setting of *Die drei Pintos*.

12. Tusa, Euryanthe, 10–11.

13. Jähns, *Carl Maria von Weber in seinen Werken*, 423.

14. Warrack, *Carl Maria von Weber*, 258. Compare the list of completed numbers (p. 258) with the outline of the opera (pp. 260–61) (as shown in my table 1). The outline of the opera is found with the sketch materials in Berlin, Deutsche Staatsbibliothek, *Weberiana*, Classe III, Band 5, No. 80.

15. Julius Benedict, *Weber*, The Great Musicians (New York: Scribner & Welford; London: Sampson, Low, Martson, Searle & Rivington, 1881), 173–74. Benedict's ideas about the completeness of the first act are tied to his knowledge of Weber's compositional method. See also Warrack, who quotes Benedict in *Carl Maria von Weber*, 258–59.

16. Weber's sketches for *Die drei Pintos* are presently located in Berlin, Deutsche Staatsbibliothek, *Weberiana*, Classe III, Band 5, No. 80. For a description of the materials, see Jähns, *Carl Maria von Weber in seinen Werken*, 417–27.

17. Benedict, *Weber*, 174. See also Warrack, *Carl Maria von Weber*, 260–61.

18. Ludwig Hartmann, *Die drei Pintos* [opera guide] (Leipzig: Hermann Seemann, [1901]), 5.

19. Reissiger worked on an arrangement of Weber's sketch no. 3 as the duet "So wie Blumen." See Jähns, *Carl Maria von Weber in seinen Werken*, 421.

20. Egon Gartenberg, *Mahler: The Man and His Music* (New York: Schirmer Books, 1978), 249.

21. References to Meyerbeer's efforts at completing *Die drei Pintos* occur in the published correspondence and diary entries. See Heinz Becker, ed., *Giacomo Meyerbeer: Briefwechsel und Tagebücher*, vol. 2, *1825–1836* (Berlin: Walter de Gruyter & Co., 1970); Heinz Becker and Gudrun Becker, eds., *Giacomo Meyerbeer: Briefwechsel und Tagebücher*, vol. 3, *1837–1845* (Berlin: Walter de Gruyter & Co., 1975); Heinz Becker and Gudrun Becker, eds., *Giacomo Meyerbeer: Briefwechsel und Tagebücher*, vol. 4, *1846–1849* (Berlin: Walter de Gruyter & Co., 1985). See also Heinz Becker's earlier article on "Meyerbeers Ergänzungsarbeit an Webers nachgelassener Oper 'Die drei Pintos,'" *Die Musikforschung* 7 (1954): 300–312.

22. See Becker, "Meyerbeers Ergänzungsarbeit," 300–312.

23. Henry-Louis de La Grange, *Mahler*, vol. 1 (Garden City, N.Y.: Doubleday and Co., 1973), 166; rev. ed., *Gustav Mahler: Chronique d'une vie*, vol. 1, *Vers la gloire 1860–1900* (Paris: Fayard, 1979), 255. The name of the composer is Vinzenz, not Franz, Lachner.

24. For an account of Mahler's career in Leipzig, including his association with Carl von Weber and his wife Marion, see La Grange, *Mahler*, 1:148–80; *Chronique d'une vie*, 1:229–75.

25. Hermann Danuser, *Gustav Mahler und seine Zeit* (Laaber: Laaber-Verlag, 1991), 122.

26. This is evident in the analysis found in Jähns, *Carl Maria von Weber in seinen Werken*, 422.

27. Natalie Bauer-Lechner, *Erinnerungen an Gustav Mahler*, edited and annotated by Knud Martner (Hamburg: Karl Dieter Wagner, 1984), 196–97; English translation, *Recollections of Gustav Mahler*, edited and annotated by Peter Franklin, translated by Dika Newlin (New York: Cambridge University Press, 1980), 176–77. The sudden inspiration in this passage has a parallel in another, later account of Mahler's sudden illumination concerning the finale for his Second Symphony; see letter of Mahler to Arthur Seidel, 17 February 1897, in Gustav Mahler, *Briefe*, edited by Herta Blaukopf (Vienna: Zsolnay, 1983), 200; English translation, *Selected Letters of Gustav Mahler*, edited by Knud Martner, translated by Eithne Wilkins, Ernst Kaiser, and Bill Hopkins (New York: Farrar, Straus & Giroux, 1979), 212.

28. See Warrack, *Carl Maria von Weber*, 263–66. With regard to Mahler's reworkings of Weber's music, see Birgit Heusgen [Braunfels], *Studien zu Gustav Mahlers Bearbeitung und Ergänzung von Carl Maria von Webers Opernfragment "Die drei Pintos,"* Kölner Beiträge zu Musikforschung, vol. 133 (Regensburg: Bosse, 1983).

29. Alma Mahler mentions that Marion von Weber worked closely with Gustav Mahler on choosing music. Alma Mahler, *Erinnerungen und Briefe* (Amsterdam: Bermann-Fischer Verlag, 1949), 140–41; English translation, *Gustav Mahler: Memories and Letters*, ed. Donald Mitchell, trans. Basil Creighton, 3rd ed. (Seattle: University of Washington Press, 1975), 110–11.

30. Dennis Phillip Davies-Wilson, "Gustav Mahler's Completion and Orchestration of *Die drei Pintos*, an Opera by Carl Maria von Weber" (master's thesis, University of New Mexico, 1991), 76–87.

31. See Hartmann's comments on Mahler's role as the "completer" (*der Ergänzer*) of the opera, in *Die drei Pintos* [opera guide], 8–9. Note also Hartmann's perspective on Mahler's affinities with Weber.

32. The Mahler family letters are part of the Gustav Mahler-Alfred Rosé Collection, University of Western Ontario, London, Ontario. Stephen McClatchie is currently preparing an edition of the letters.

33. Gustav Mahler to his parents, 7 September 1887, Gustav Mahler-Alfred Rosé Collection, shelfmark E2-MFp-58.

34. Gustav Mahler to his parents, 4 October 1887, Gustav Mahler-Alfred Rosé Collection, shelfmark E2-MFp-59.

35. Gustav Mahler to his parents, 7 November 1887, Gustav Mahler-Alfred Rosé Collection, shelfmark E2-MF-72. I am indebted to Stephen McClatchie for his dating of this letter.

36. Gustav Mahler to his parents, Gustav Mahler-Alfred Rosé Collection, shelfmark E2-MF-60.

37. Gustav Mahler to his parents, Gustav Mahler-Alfred Rosé Collection, shelfmark E2-MF-55; see also Gustav Mahler, *Briefe*, ed. Herta Blaukopf (Vienna: Zsolnay, 1983), 65.

38. Gustav Mahler to his parents, 21 January 1888, Gustav Mahler-Alfred Rosé Collection, shelfmark E13-MF-540. See also Mahler, *Briefe*, 68–69.

39. *Mahler*, 1:148–80; *Chronique d'une vie*, 1:229–82.

40. Hanslick, "Die drei Pintos," 94–95.

41. Ibid., 89.

42. La Grange, *Mahler*, 1:170; *Chronique d'une vie*, 1:259–61. See also Herta Blaukopf, ed., *Gustav Mahler / Richard Strauss: Briefwechsel 1888–1911* (Munich: Piper, 1980), 137–39; English translation, *Gustav Mahler / Richard Strauss: Correspondence 1888–1911*, trans. Edmund Jephcott (Chicago: University of Chicago Press, 1984), 107–9.

43. Quoted by Herta Blaukopf, *Briefwechsel 1888–1911*, 138; *Correspondence 1888–1911*, 108.

44. Gustav Mahler to Richard Batka, 18 November 1896, in Mahler, *Briefe*, 179; English translation, *Selected Letters of Gustav Mahler*, 197.

45. Gustav Mahler to Max Marschalk, [4] December 1896, in *Briefe*, 183; *Selected Letters*, 200.

46. Bauer-Lechner, *Erinnerungen*, 196–97; *Recollections*, 176–77.

47. Guido Adler, "Gustav Mahler," in Edward R. Reilly, *Gustav Mahler and Guido Adler: Records of a Friendship* (New York: Cambridge University Press, 1982), 32; originally published in Guido Adler, *Gustav Mahler* (Vienna: Universal-Edition, 1916), 12–13. Reilly's Cambridge publication (including his essay on Mahler and Adler) appeared in German first as *Gustav Mahler und Guido Adler: Zur Geschichte einer Freundschaft*, Bibliothek der Internationalen Gustav Mahler Gesellschaft (Vienna: Universal Edition, 1978).

48. Bauer-Lechner, *Erinnerungen*, 197; *Recollections*, 177.

49. See Lydia Goehr, *The Imaginary Museum of Musical Works: An Essay in the Philosophy of Music* (Oxford: Clarendon Press, 1994), 256.

50. The first publication concerned with *Die drei Pintos* is the guide by Ludwig Hartmann, op. cit. It is useful to note that the title page and page headers of this publication refer to the work as Weber's without including Mahler's name anywhere except in the body of the text (the header on recto pages reads "Carl Maria von Weber: 'Die drei Pintos' "). No reference to Mahler's involvement with the opera occurs in Richard Specht, *Gustav Mahler* (Berlin: Schuster & Loeffler, 1913), despite his extensive treatment of Mahler as opera director (pp. 63–154), and the list of *Bearbeitungen* published at the end of Specht's book contains only *Oberon*. As to Paul Bekker's later study, the title obviates extended reference to the opera; see Bekker, *Gustav Mahlers Sinfonien* (Berlin: Schuster & Loeffler, 1921; reprint, Tutzing: Hans Schneider, 1969). Yet Guido Adler, op. cit., mentions without apology *Die drei Pintos* in the context of the composer's life and work. It is significant that as late as 1984, the principal Mahler biography by Henry-Louis de La Grange includes *Die drei Pintos* in the appendices under the rubric "Versions et retouches." See *Gustav Mahler: Chronique d'une vie*, vol. 3, *la génie foudroyé 1907–1911* (Paris: Fayard, 1984), 1267–74.

51. For a comprehensive list of Mahler's *Bearbeitungen*, see Susan M. Filler, *Gustav and Alma Mahler: A Guide to Research* (New York: Garland Publishing, 1989), xliii–xlvii; see also Bruno and Eleonore Vondenhoff, *Gustav Mahler Dokumentation: Materialien zu Leben und Werk* (Tutzing, Hans Schneider, 1978), 444–54 ("Bearbeitungen").

52. For a discussion of *Bearbeitungen* from an editorial and philological perspective, see Georg Feder, *Musikphilologie: Eine Einführung in die musikalische Textkritik, Hermeneutik und Editions-*

technik (Darmstadt: Wissenschaftliche Buchgesellschaft, 1987), 155–56.

53. "Intégrale Gustav Mahler: Symphonies, Lieder," 10 February to 10 May 1989, Châtelet, Théâtre musical de Paris. The concert performance of *Die drei Pintos* took place on 23 March 1989. See the program book, *Intégrale Gustav Mahler: Symphonies, Lieder* (Paris: Fondation Société Générale pour la Musique, [1989]), 103–9.

54. The concept of an *Ausgabe letzter Hand* or *Fassung letzter Hand* can be problematic with regard to Mahler's music. For a consideration of this issue for one work of Mahler, see James L. Zychowicz, "Toward an *Ausgabe letzter hand:* The Publication and Revision of Mahler's Fourth Symphony," *Journal of Musicology* 12 (1995): 260–72.

55. Gartenberg, *Mahler*, 249.

56. Carl Maria von Weber and Gustav Mahler, *Die drei Pintos: Komische Oper in drei Aufzügen,* conducted by Gary Bertini, notes by F. Willnauer (RCA: PRL3 9063, 1977 [LP]; 74321-32246-2 [CD, released 1995]).

Libretto and Translation

The source of the libretto is *Die drei Pintos: Komische Oper in drei Aufzügen*, by C. M. von Weber (Leipzig: C. F. Kahnt, 1888), which is reproduced here with an English translation. In listing the title in this manner, Carl Maria von Weber is given credit for the opera, and the nature of the completion occurs lower on the title page, with the description stated as it occurs in the lithograph score: "Unter Zugrundelegung des gleichnamigen Textbuches von Th[eodor] Hell, der hinterlassenen Entwürfe und ausgewählter Manuscripte des Componisten ausgeführt: der dramatische Theil von Carl von Weber, der musikalische von Gustav Mahler." Credit is thereby given to Weber's grandson for his part in revising the libretto, with the musical completion left to Mahler.

As to the libretto, the German text retains the orthography of the source, including the original spellings (for example, *Theil* rather than the modern *Teil*, etc.). A similar effort has been made to preserve the punctuation of the source, including punctuation which surrounds dashes in the spoken dialogue. The capitalization of the German text has been regularized such that each line of poetic passages, that is, the sung text, is capitalized. For spoken dialogue, this edition uses prose style. Abbreviations, when they occur in the source, are spelled out in this edition.

As to other elements, directions, when they occur, are regularized and rendered in italics within parentheses. The source includes the indication "Dialog" for spoken text, and this element is included in the edition. The order of headings for scenes, characters, number titles, and dialogue passages has been regularized throughout. Names of characters are given in capital letters to distinguish the speakers from the text itself. With regard to the numbering of the musical sections, the libretto differs from the lithograph score and the piano-vocal score in having the duet and trio both as "No. 11 Duett und Terzett"; from there the numbers listed in the libretto are off by one. In this edition, the numbering of the libretto has been made to match that of the musical sources.

In general, the text of the libretto corresponds to the score. Where they occur, differences concern punctuation along with some rewordings. An effort has been made to follow the text source and not to collate it with the text of the score. However, a few longer passages of the score that are not found in the text source are included with the edition of the libretto. These passages are set off with brackets in both the German text and English translation.

The translation uses prose capitalization for both the sung text and spoken dialogue. In the sung text, an attempt has been made to have the translation of each new line correspond to the original German line, but the translation is not intended to be sung.

Personen

Don Pantaleone Roiz de Pacheco ⎫
Don Gomez Freiros   ⎬ Edelleute zu Madrid
Clarissa, Don Pantaleone's Tochter
Laura, Clarissen's Zofe
Don Gaston Viratos, ehemals Student zu Salamanca
Don Pinto de Fonseca, ein junger Landedelmann aus Castilla

Characters

Don Pantaleone Roiz de Pacheco ⎫
Don Gomez Freiros   ⎬ Nobles of Madrid
Clarissa, Don Pantaleone's daughter
Laura, Clarissa's maid
Don Gaston Viratos, erstwhile student at Salamanca
Don Pinto de Fonseca, a young country squire from Castille

Der Wirth der Dorfschänke zu Peñaranda	The Innkeeper of the village inn at Peñaranda
Inez, dessen Tochter	Inez, his daughter
Ambrosio, Don Gaston's Diener	Ambrosio, Don Gaston's servant
Der Haushofmeister Don Pantaleone's	The Steward of Don Pantaleone
Studenten von Salamanca	Students from Salamanca
Dienerschaft im Hause Don Pantaleone's und in der Dorfschänke zu Peñaranda	Servants in Don Pantaleone's house and in the village inn at Peñaranda

Ort der Handlung

1. Aufzug: In der Dorfschänke zu Peñaranda, halbwegs zwischen Salamanca und Madrid
2. und 3. Aufzug: Im Hause Don Pantaleone's zu Madrid

Erster Aufzug

(*Der Veranda vor der Dorf-Schänke zu Peñaranda. Dieselbe stößt an das Haus, welches die linke Hälfte des Prospectes ausmacht, Türen führen in dasselbe. Man sieht aus der Veranda nach rückwärts in's Freie.*)

Scene 1

Studenten aus Salamanca sind beim Gelage versammelt. Unter ihnen Don Gaston Viratos und sein Diener Ambrosio. Der Wirt.

No. 1. Chor

CHOR

Leeret die Becher,
Mutige Zecher,
Bis auf den Grund!
Tagen der Freude,
Folgen nun heute
Trennung und Leid.
Nie zu vergessen,
Was wir besessen,
Sei heut' geschworen!

GASTON

Reicht mir den größten Becher her,
Die Euren nehmt zu Händen,
Auf Salamanca trinkt sie leer
Und seine Herr'n Studenten!
Auf ewig bleib' sie frisch und grün,
Die Jugendkraft, die Jugendkraft,
Die alles kühne Streben
Zum höchsten Ziel muß heben!

CHOR

Auf ewig bleib' sie frisch und grün,
Die Jugendkraft, die Jugendkraft,
Die unser kühnes Streben
Zum höchsten Ziel muß heben!
Hurrah!
Sie lebe hoch!

AMBROSIO

(*tanzend*)
Lalalala! Lalalala!

Scene of the Action

Act 1: In the village inn at Peñaranda, halfway between Salamanca and Madrid
Acts 2 and 3: At Don Pantaleone's house in Madrid

Act One

(*The veranda in front of the tavern in Peñaranda. The latter abuts the house, the left half of which creates a perspective with towers bordering the same. One sees from the veranda open spaces in the distance.*)

Scene 1

Students from Salamanca are drinking together. Among them are Don Gaston Viratos, his servant Ambrosio, and the Innkeeper.

No. 1. Chorus

CHORUS

Empty the goblets,
cheerful companions,
to the last.
After today,
parting and pain
follow days of joy.
Do not forget,
what we possessed,
may it be sworn today!

GASTON

Give me the largest goblet,
take yours in your hands,
empty them to Salamanca
and its honorable students!
May it always remain fresh and green,
the strength of youth,
that lifts all our aspirations
to the highest goal!

CHORUS

May it always remain fresh and green,
the strength of youth,
that lifts all our aspirations
to the highest goal!
Hurray!
Long may it live!

AMBROSIO

(*dancing*)
Lalalala! Lalalala!

(*bei Seite*)
Es lebe der Wein!
Es lebe das Glück!

CHOR

Leeret die Becher,
Mutige Zecher!
Bis auf den Grund!
(*Sie umdrängen Gaston.*)
Bruder, dir weihe
Heut' ich aufs Neue
Freundschaft und Lieb',
Innig verbunden.
Haben uns Stunden
Seligster Lust!

GASTON

Nun Freunde reicht mir Eure Hand
Zum letzten Abschiedsgruße.
Ich ziehe meinen Weg durch's Land,
Ihr kehrt zurück zur Muse.
Doch rufen wir voll Hoffnung aus:
Auf Wiederseh'n! Auf Wiederseh'n!
Mit Gottes reichstem Segen
Heil, Heil auf allen Wegen!

CHOR

Doch rufen wir voll Hoffnung aus:
Auf Wiederseh'n! Auf Wiederseh'n!
Mit Gottes reichstem Segen
Heil, Heil auf allen Wegen!
Auf Wiederseh'n!
Selbst in der Trennung Schmerz
Tönet d'rum lauter Scherz.
Jubelt, la la!
Nochmals zum Scheidegruß tönet es laut:
Auf Wiederseh'n!

(*Sie brechen geräuschvoll auf, ordnen sich zu Zuge und ziehen durch die offene Seite der Veranda ab. Man hört ihren Gesang draußen allmälig verklingen. Don Gaston blickt ihnen sinnend nach.*)

Dialog

GASTON

Also vorbei—fröhliche, selige Studentenzeit! Und—auch vorbei die Jugend? He, Ambrosio, sag, hast du nicht einen guten Einfall, der mir über diesen Abschied hinweghilft?

AMBROSIO

Hier, in diesem Wirtshaus gute Einfälle! Herr, wollen wir nicht weiter?

GASTON

Hast recht, Ambrosio, weiter nach Madrid!

AMBROSIO

Ach, in Madrid, Herr, das schwör' ich Euch, da sollen mir mehr tolle Streiche einfallen als Ihr ausführen könnt.

(*aside*)
Long live the wine!
Long live good fortune!

CHORUS

Empty the goblets,
cheerful companions,
to the last!
(*They surround Gaston.*)
Brother, to you I dedicate
today, again,
friendship and love,
closely bound.
We have for ourselves hours
of blessed happiness!

GASTON

Now, friends, give me your hands
for the final leave-taking.
I make my way into the country,
you return to the muse.
Yet we call out full of hope:
Farewell! Farewell!
With God's fullest blessing,
hail on all our paths!

CHORUS

We call out full of hope:
Farewell! Farewell!
With God's fullest blessing,
hail on all our paths!
Farewell!
Therefore, even in the sorrow of
parting, banter resounds.
Rejoice, la la!
Once again, for the leave-taking, say it loudly:
Farewell!

(*They break up noisily, file out, and leave through the open side of the veranda. One hears their song outside gradually die away. Don Gaston looks at them pensively.*)

Dialogue

GASTON

So it is gone—blissful, happy student days! And also gone is youth? Hey, Ambrosio, tell me, have you a good plan which can rid me of the good-bye?

AMBROSIO

Here, in this inn, good plans! Sir, don't you want to go further?

GASTON

You're right, Ambrosio, further to Madrid!

AMBROSIO

Ah, in Madrid, sir, I promise you that I should think of more crazy pranks than you can carry out.

GASTON
In Madrid, mein Junge, da wirst du die Akten hinter mir d'reintragen, und ich werde den Corregidor Stab führen—und nun ruf den Wirt mit seiner Rechnung her!

AMBROSIO
Hahaha! Das ist zum Lachen! Ihr Corregidor!

GASTON
Das ist sehr ernst, Du Galgenstrick. Nun ruf' den Wirth mit seiner Rechnung her!

AMBROSIO
(*im Abgehen*) O weh, o weh, bezahlen!

GASTON
Ihr schönen, goldenen Dublonen—habt ihr geahnt, daß ihr euch in diesem sauren Landwein auflösen würdet? Bis auf den Letzten!—Was aber dann?

Scene 2

Don Gaston, Ambrosio

No. 2. Rondo
GASTON
Was ich dann thu', das frag' ich mich,
Frag' ich denn nicht recht wunderlich?
Ich such' ein Mädchen, das mich liebt,
Das mir sein holdes Herzlein giebt
Doch wenn sie meine Hand verschmäht?
Wenn ihr Herz nach 'nem Andern steht?
Wenn sie nach spröder Weiber Art
Fest auf ihrem Sinn beharrt?
Was ich dann thu', das frag' ich mich,
Frag' ich denn nicht recht wunderlich?
Sprech' bei einer Andern vor,
Die leiht mir geneigtes Ohr!
Wahrlich, wahrlich, ja, das thu' ich,
Mädchen, ja ganz sicherlich!
Seid Ihr hübsch und jung und reich,
Seid Ihr vor mir Alle gleich,
Seid Ihr doch vor mir gleich!
D'rum schöne Mädchen hütet Euch!

Dialog
AMBROSIO
Hier ist der Mann mit der Rechnung. Herr, oder vielmehr die Rechnung mit dem Manne, denn sie ist zehnmal so lang, wie er!

GASTON
Zeig' her, Du Wirth, der bei unserm Beutel zu Gast ist! Und Du, Ambrosio, stell' Dich hinter mich, und halte mich wenn ich umfalle!

WIRTH
Ich habe, bei meiner Seele, die allernidrigsten Preise angesetzt—

GASTON
In Madrid, young man, you will carry documents after me, and I will hold the Corregidor's staff — now call the innkeeper for the bill.

AMBROSIO
Hahaha! That's laughable! You as the Corregidor!

GASTON
I'm serious, you rascal. Now call the innkeeper for the bill.

AMBROSIO
(*leaving*) Oh dear, oh dear—to pay!

GASTON
You beautiful, golden doubloons—did you have any idea that you would be spent on a sour, humble vintage? Down to the last doubloons!—What then?

Scene 2

Don Gaston, Ambrosio

No. 2. Rondo
GASTON
What will I do then, I ask myself,
am I asking a strange question?
I search for a maiden, who loves me,
who gives me her dear little heart,
what if she shuns my hand?
If her heart belongs to another?
If, according to the reticent way
that women have, she remains unmoved?
What will I do then, I ask myself,
am I asking a strange question?
I will approach another,
who inclines an ear to me!
Truly, truly, I will do that!
Maiden, that will be so!
If you are cute and young and rich,
you are all the same to me,
truly, you are all the same to me!
Therefore be on your guard, Maidens!

Dialogue
AMBROSIO
Here is the man with the bill. Sir, I should say the bill with the man, since it is ten times taller than he.

GASTON
Bring it here, innkeeper, who is a guest of my wallet! And you, Ambrosio, stand behind me and hold me when I fall!

INNKEEPER
I have, by my soul, given you the lowest possible prices—

GASTON
Und doch ist, die Summe so hoch wie ein Haus, Du verflixter Rechenkünstler! Heilige Mutter von Urgel—Das soll ich bezahlen? Ambrosio—mein letzter Heller!

AMBROSIO
Ei, ei, ei, ei.

WIRTH
Ei, ei!

Scene 3

Der Vorige, [Gaston], Ambrosio, Wirth

No. 3. Terzett

GASTON
Ei, ei, ei!
Wer hätte das gedacht,
Hab' ich an einem Tage
Mein Geld total verpufft!

Ei, ei, ei!
Was liegt denn viel daran:
Hab' ich nur gute Laune,
Was kränkt mich dann das Geld?

AMBROSIO
Ei!
Wer hätte das gedacht,
Hat er an einem Tage
Sein Geld total verpufft!

Ei!
Was liegt denn viel daran:
Hat er nur gute Laune,
Was kränkt ihn dann das Geld?

WIRTH
[Ei, ei, ei,
Wer hätte das gedacht!
Dass ich an frühem Tage
Sein Geld im Sache hätt'!]

Ei, ei, ei!
Da liegt mir viel daran:
Ist er bei guter Laune,
Was kränkt ihn dann das Geld?

Dialog

GASTON
Nun hier, Du Straßenräuber, hier hast Du Deinen Sündenlohn! (*Er zahlt.*)

WIRTH
Sauer verdient, Herr, sauer verdient!

GASTON
And yet the sum is truly as high as this house, you confounded mathematician! Holy mother of Urgel—I should pay that? Ambrosio, my last cent!

AMBROSIO
Oh, oh, oh, oh.

INNKEEPER
Oh, oh!

Scene 3

As before, [Gaston], Ambrosio, Innkeeper

No. 3. Trio

GASTON
Oh, oh, oh!
Who would have thought it,
I have in a single day
completely spent my money!

Oh, oh, oh!
What does it really matter:
If only I am in a good mood,
why should money bother me?

AMBROSIO
Oh!
Who would have thought it,
he has in a single day
completely spent his money!

Oh!
What does it really matter:
If only he has a good mood,
why should money bother him?

INNKEEPER
[Oh, oh, oh,
who could have thought it!
I have in a single day
his money in my pocket!]

Oh, oh, oh!
What does it really matter:
If only he is in a good mood,
why should money bother him?

Dialogue

GASTON
Now here, you highway-robber, here, you have your blood money! (*He pays.*)

INNKEEPER
Bitterly earned, sir, bitterly earned!

GASTON
Ja, Du Schuft, mit saurem Weine und mit saurer Miene.

WIRTH
(*pfiffig*) O meine gnädigen Herren, ich habe auch gar süße Weine—wollt Ihr's versuchen?

GASTON
Nun bei Gott, ein guter Gedanke! (*Er greift in die Tasche und bringt einige Goldstücke hervor.*)

WIRTH
(*ab*)

AMBROSIO
Herr, wir sollten aber doch nicht so eilig hier fortgehen—ich sage Euch, der Wirth hat eine Tochter—

GASTON
Du Blitzjunge, wie hast Du dies so schnell entdeckt?

AMBROSIO
Ei nun, Herr, so in Küche und Keller herum, wie sich's für den Diener schickt!

GASTON
Und warum hab' ich sie noch nicht gesehen? Sie soll kommen, sofort erscheinen! Wie heißt der Engel, Ambrosio?

AMBROSIO
Inez, Euer Gnaden!

GASTON
Inez? Schon dieser Name enzündet mich! Herbei mit ihr! Fort, Ambrosio! (*Als Ambrosio abgehen will, hört man die Klänge einer Guitarre.*)

AMBROSIO
Beim Himmel, Herr, da sitzt sie und hebt zu singen an!

GASTON
Ein reizendes Wesen!

No. 4. Romanze
INEZ
(*hinter der Scene singend*)
Leise weht' es, leise wallte
Rings der Thau herab,
Als im nächt'gen Grau der Kater Mansor
Hin den Pfad der Liebe schlich.

Dialog
GASTON
Was singt sie? Der Kater Mansor?

AMBROSIO
Bei Gott, vom Kater Mansor. Der macht Euch sicher verliebte Streiche!

GASTON
Yes, you scoundrel, with bitter wine and a bitter countenance.

INNKEEPER
(*craftily*) My gracious sirs, I have truly sweet wines—would you like to try?

GASTON
Now, by God, a good thought! (*He reaches into the wallet and brings out several gold coins.*)

INNKEEPER
(*within*)

AMBROSIO
Sir, we should not leave this place so quickly—I tell you, the innkeeper has a daughter—

GASTON
Bright one, how did you discover this so fast?

AMBROSIO
Well, sir, in the kitchen and cellar as is appropriate for a servant.

GASTON
And why haven't I seen her yet. She should come forward and appear right away. What's the angel's name, Ambrosio?

AMBROSIO
Inez, your grace!

GASTON
Inez? This name inflames me already! Bring her here! Forward, Ambrosio! (*As Ambrosio goes inside, the sound of a guitar is heard.*)

AMBROSIO
By heaven, sir, she's sitting there and about to sing!

GASTON
A charming creature!

No. 4. Romanza
INEZ
(*singing behind the stage*)
Softly the breezes blow,
softly, the dew falls,
as Tomcat Mansor, in the evening's grayness,
creeps on the path of love.

Dialogue
GASTON
What's she singing? "Kater Mansor," the tomcat?

AMBROSIO
By God, of "Kater Mansor." He probably makes very romantic pranks for you!

INEZ
(*singt*)
Einzeln, recht nach seinem Herzen
Stand das Häuschen da,
Das Zaïden, sein geliebtes,
Bestes Katzen Mädchen barg.
(*Während der Romanze bringt der Wirth Wein und Gläser.*)

Dialog
GASTON UND AMBROSIO
(*in die Hände klatschend*) Herrlich, wundervoll!

GASTON
Herein, herein! Herbei Du hold Kätzlein! Singe hier! Hier bei Deinem treuen Kater Mansor!

Scene 4.

Vorige. Inez (tritt in die Veranda herein; sie macht Gaston einen Knix).

Dialog
INEZ
Wollt Ihr der Kater Mansor sein, Herr Ritter?

GASTON
Wenn Du mein Kätzchen sein willst!

INEZ
So hört die traurige Geschichte erst zu Ende!
(*singt*)
Leise weht' es, leise wallte
Rings der Thau herab,
Als der falsche, harte Kater Mansor
Glühend, ew'ge Treue schwur.
Doch beim Morgenstrahle flieht er,
Flieht auf immer,
Ach Zaïden, und ihr Herz
Voll Lieb' in Katzen-Jammer bricht!

Dialog
GASTON UND AMBROSIO
Bravo, bravo, unvergleichlich!

GASTON
Aber Pfui über den abscheulichen, treulosen Kater!

INEZ
Der seid doch Ihr, Herr Ritter!

GASTON
Wie, ich der treulose, Kater Mansor?

INEZ
Sagtet Ihr's nicht selbst?

GASTON
O Du Schelmin! Dir wär' ich sicher treu!

INEZ
(*sings*)
Alone, right after his heart,
stood the little house,
which hid his Zaïde, his beloved,
the best girl-cat.
(*During the Romanza, the innkeeper brings wine and glasses.*)

Dialogue
GASTON AND AMBROSIO
(*clapping their hands*) Great! Wonderful!

GASTON
Here, here! Here, you dear little cat. Sing again! Here, for your own true Tomcat Mansor!

Scene 4

As before. Inez (steps onto the veranda; she curtsies to Gaston).

Dialogue
INEZ
Would you want to be the Tomcat Mansor, sir knight?

GASTON
Only if you would be my kitten!

INEZ
So listen to the sad story from beginning to end!
(*sings*)
Softly the breezes blow,
softly, the dew falls,
when the false, hard Kater Mansor,
glowing, swears eternal faith.
Yet at the break of dawn he flees,
flees forever,
oh, Zaïde, and her heart
full of love, breaks in the realization of the morning after.

Dialogue
GASTON AND AMBROSIO
Bravo, bravo! Incomparable!

GASTON
But phooey on the horrible, faithless tomcat!

INEZ
Yet he is you, sir knight!

GASTON
What, I am the faithless Kater Mansor?

INEZ
Didn't you say so yourself?

GASTON
You poor trickster! To you would I certainly be true!

INEZ Wie Kater Mansor?	**INEZ** As true as Kater Mansor?
GASTON Willst Du's versuchen?	**GASTON** Do you want to try?
INEZ Beileibe nicht!	**INEZ** Not at all!
GASTON Ich biete Dir mich selbst zum Pfand—mich, Deinen Gaston.	**GASTON** I offer myself as a pledge, me, your Gaston.
INEZ Und was soll ich dagegen geben, Don Mansor?	**INEZ** And what should I give for that, Don Mansor?
GASTON Nichts als Dich selbst und zehn, hundert, tausend Küsse!	**GASTON** Nothing but yourself and ten, a hundred, a thousand kisses!
INEZ Da müßt' ich doch erst wissen, ob Ihr so viel wert seid, werter Herr!	**INEZ** I must first know if you would be worth so much, worthy sir!
GASTON Ich bin noch mehr wert.	**GASTON** I am worth even more.
INEZ Man ist das wert, was man ist. Nun denn, Herr, was seid Ihr?	**INEZ** You are worth what you are worth. Now then, sir, what are you?
GASTON Nun beim Himmel, —ich bin—ich bin—ich war Student!	**GASTON** Now, by heaven, —I am—I am—I was a student!
INEZ (*lachend*) Ei, was Ihr seid, Herr!	**INEZ** (*laughing*) Oh, so you are, sir!
GASTON Ich bin auch noch Student, denn ein Student bleibt ewig Student. Weißt Du was das heißt, hold Inez, Student?	**GASTON** I am even now a student, for one always remains a student. Do you know what that means, dear Inez, to be a student?
INEZ Nun, so ziemlich! Lustig, durstig, verliebt, beutelarm!	**INEZ** Now, possibly! Merry, thirsty, in love, and poor!
GASTON Kind, der Student ist Alles!—er kann es wenigstens Alles werden!	**GASTON** Child, a student is everything!—at least he can become anything.
No. 5. Canzonette (Seguidilla a dos)	No. 5. Canzonette (Seguidilla a dos)
GASTON Wir, die den Musen dienen, Sind auch den Grazien hold. Wir stehen wohl bei Jenen, Doch die bei uns im Sold. Und unser ganzes Leben Ist ihnen hingegeben Mit heißer Leidenschaft!	**GASTON** We, who serve the muses, are also dear to the graces. We are beholden to them, just as they are beholden to us. And our entire lives are given to them with intense passion.
INEZ Doch nie, daß es Euch Leiden schafft!	**INEZ** Yet never that it in such a way gives you pain!

GASTON
Wenn's gilt, mit Männern streiten,
Wir schlagen rasch darein,
Doch sind wir gegen Frauen
Allzeit gar zart und fein.
D'rum lieben uns die Mädchen
In jedem Dorf und Städtchen,
Wo wir uns lassen seh'n!

INEZ
Ja, wenn Sie schleunigst wieder geh'n!

GASTON
Zwar leben wir in Freuden,
Bei Sang und Rebensaft,
Doch wirkt in uns die Weisheit
Auch mit besond'rer Kraft.
In aller Musen Tempel
Wir nennen uns Exempel
Der höchsten Wissenschaft!

INEZ
Ei, wie gewissenhaft!

GASTON
D'rum leben die Studenten—!

INEZ
Da's einmal denn muß sein!

GASTON
Es lebe, was sie lieben—!

INEZ
Das geb' ich auch noch d'rein!

GASTON
D'rum, Mädchen, sollst Du leben,
Dir ist mein Herz ergeben:
Dich oder Keine lieb' ich mehr!

INEZ
Mein Herr Student, ich danke sehr!

Dialog

AMBROSIO
Herr, Herr, um's Himmelswillen schauen Sie her, schauen Sie her!

INEZ UND GASTON
Was gibt's, was gibt's?

AMBROSIO
Ist das nicht der Mühe wert? Hahaha!

GASTON
Wie sich der Kerl vom Pferde wälzt—!

INEZ
Da gibt's zu tun—verzeiht, mein Herr Student. (*ab*)

GASTON
When necessary, we fight with men,
and strike quickly,
yet when it comes to women
we are always tender and refined.
Thus the maidens love us
in every village and town,
wherever we are seen!

INEZ
Especially when you leave quickly!

GASTON
To be sure we truly live in bliss,
by song and wine,
yet wisdom grows in us
with exceptional strength.
In all the muses' temples
we call ourselves examples
of the highest wisdom!

INEZ
Oh, how conscientious!

GASTON
Therefore students live—!

INEZ
Since they have to do so!

GASTON
Vivat! What they love—!

INEZ
That much I'll give you!

GASTON
Thus, maiden, you should live,
to you I give my heart;
you and no one else do I love any more!

INEZ
My lord student, I thank you much!

Dialogue

AMBROSIO
Sir, sir, for heaven's sakes, look here, look here!

INEZ AND GASTON
What's up, what's up?

AMBROSIO
Isn't it worth the bother? Hahaha!

GASTON
How that fellow stumbles off his horse—!

INEZ
There's something to do—pardon, my lord student. (*leaves*)

AMBROSIO
Herr, wenn der uns nicht Spaß für den ganzen Tag schafft, will ich mein Lebtag das Maul nicht mehr zum Lachen verziehen! O, wie er prustet nach dieser Arbeit!

GASTON
Seiner Kleidung nach ein Landedelmann!

AMBROSIO
Ja, er scheint auf einem Gutshofe auf Fett gezüchtet zu sein!

GASTON
Bei Gott, er kommt hierher—Ambrosio, heut' soll's noch lustig werden!

Scene 5

Gaston, Ambrosio, Don Pinto

DIALOG

PINTO
(*im Eintreten*) Braten und kochen, backen und sieden! Ich habe einen Riesen-Appetit und zahle was Ihr wollt! Uff! uff! (*Er grüßt Gaston wegwerfend und setzt sich auf einen Stuhl.*) Bei allen Heiligen, das ist eine Reise! Von Castilla hierher in einem Tage! Wenn nicht unterwegs ein paar Gasthäuser wären—Uff! uff! Die Hitze—der Hunger und der Durst! (*Er schlägt auf den Tisch.*) Ich will trinken—He, Wein her! Wein her!

GASTON
Ambrosio, schnell, sorg' für den Ritter; er hat Durst! Schnell, Wein vom Besten!

PINTO
(*dummstolz*) Seid Ihr der Wirt?

GASTON
Leider, nein. Um solch eines Gastes willen, möcht' ich's wohl gern sein. Ich bin ein Ritter, wie Ihr!

PINTO
Ein Ritter, ah ein Ritter! War der Anderer auch ein Ritter?

GASTON
Nein, der war mein Diener, Euch zu dienen, Herr Ritter.

PINTO
Verzeiht—ich mein es sähe Einer wie der Andere aus!—Hahaha!

GASTON
Hahah! Sehr guter Witz. Castilla ist, wie mir scheint, eine sehr witzige Stadt.

PINTO
Woher wißt Ihr, daß ich aus Castilla bin?

AMBROSIO
Sir, if he's not going to make us laugh for an entire day, I should not laugh for the rest of my life. Oh, how he's winded after his labor!

GASTON
He is dressed like a country squire!

AMBROSIO
Yes, he seems fattened on a farm!

GASTON
By God, he's coming here—Ambrosio, today we should have some merriment!

Scene 5

Gaston, Ambrosio, Don Pinto.

DIALOGUE

PINTO
(*entering*) Roast and cook, bake and boil! I have a gigantic appetite and will pay whatever you want! Uff! Uff! (*He greets Gaston condescendingly and sits on a chair.*) By all the saints, that's a journey! From Castille to here in a single day! If it were not for a couple of inns along the way—Uff! Uff! The heat—hunger and thirst! (*He bangs on the table.*) I want something to drink—hey! wine here! Wine here!

GASTON
Ambrosio, quick, take care of the knight; he's thirsty! Fast, the best wine!

PINTO
(*arrogantly*) Are you the innkeeper?

GASTON
Sorry, no. Though for such a guest, I would very much like to be. I am a knight like you!

PINTO
A knight, ah, a knight! Was the other one a knight, too?

GASTON
No, he was my servant, and will serve you, sir knight.

PINTO
Pardon, I think that one looks like the other—hahaha!

GASTON
Hahah! A very good joke. Castille, it seems to be a very funny town.

PINTO
How do you know that I am from Castille?

GASTON Ihr habt's ja selbst gesagt!	GASTON You told me yourself!
PINTO Ich hab's gesagt?—Zu Euch?	PINTO I said so? To you?
GASTON Nein, Herr Ritter, zu Euch!	GASTON No, sir knight, to you!
PINTO Zu mir?—Hahaha!	PINTO To me?—Hahaha!
GASTON Ja, zu Euch? Hahah!	GASTON Yes, to you? Hahah!
PINTO Nun bei allen Heiligen, Ihr gefallt mir, Herr Ritter!	PINTO Now, by all the saints, you please me, sir knight!
GASTON Nicht besser, als Ihr mir, Don Augustino!	GASTON None better than you please me, Don Augustino!
PINTO Woher wißt Ihr, daß ich Don Augustino heiße?	PINTO How do you know that I am called Don Augustino?
GASTON Heißt Ihr denn so?	GASTON You are called that?
PINTO Nein, ich heiße nicht Don Augustino.	PINTO No, I am not called Don Augustino.
GASTON Hahaha!	GASTON Hahaha!
PINTO Hahaha!—Nun müßt Ihr mir aber sagen, wie Ihr heißt.	PINTO Hahaha!—Now you must tell me how you're called.
GASTON Ich heiße Don Gaston Viratos.	GASTON I am named Don Gaston Viratos.
PINTO Don Gaston Viratos? Nun denn, so will ich Euch auch meinen Namen nennen. Ich heiße Don Pinto de Fonseca.	PINTO Don Gaston Viratos? Now then, I will also tell you my name. I am called Don Pinto de Fonseca.
GASTON Ach, ein edler Name!	GASTON Ah, a noble name!
PINTO Wie meint Ihr das, Don Gaston?	PINTO How do you mean that, Don Gaston?
GASTON Ich meine, es muß ein edler Name sein, den ein Edelmann von Eurer Erscheinung trägt.	GASTON I mean that it must be a noble name, that a nobleman of your appearance bears.
PINTO Ihr habt Recht, Don Gaston! Was werdet Ihr aber dazu sagen, daß ich diesem uralten Namen, dessen letzter Träger ich bin, einen noch urälteren hinzuzufügen gedenke?	PINTO You are right, Don Gaston! What would you say that I, of that ancient name and of which I am the last bearer, if I were to add an even older name to it?
GASTON Was ich sagen würde?—Ich bin stumm vor Erstaunen!	GASTON What would I say? I am speechless from astonishment!

PINTO
Ja, ja, Don Gaston, ich werde ein Mädchen heiraten.

GASTON
Mein' Seel'—ein Mädchen?

PINTO
Die Letzte aus dem Stamme der Pacheco's zu Madrid. Dann nennen wir uns Fonseca y Pancheco!

AMBROSIO
(*hat inzwischen Wein gebracht, von dem Pinto schnell und viel trinkt*)

GASTON
Das klingt gar herrlich—meinen Glückwunsch, edler Don zu Eurer Verlobung.

PINTO
Ja, Glück könnt Ihr mir wünschen! Donna Clarissa ist schön, reich und liebenswürdig—

GASTON
Ihr Glücklicher!

PINTO
Das heißt, ich habe sie noch nie gesehen, aber mein Vater sagt es, der mir befohlen hat, sie zu heiraten.

GASTON
Befohlen?

PINTO
Ja, die Sache ist zwischen beiden Vätern abgemacht. Sie sind Jugendfreunde und mein Vater hat meinem zukünftigen Schwiegervater einmal—(*Er saft Don Gaston etwas in's Ohr.*)

GASTON
(*erstaunt*) Ah!

PINTO
Ja, ja! Und nun soll ich zum Dank dafür seine Tochter Clarissa zum Weibe erhalten. Ja, ja, ja! Seht Ihr, und nun reise ich mit dem Briefe meines Vaters nach Madrid. (*Er holt einen Brief hervor.*) Hier ist er! Was mag da wohl drinnen steh'n?

GASTON
Das kann ich Euch nicht sagen!

PINTO
Schade, schade!—Ei, der alte Pacheco wird Augen machen, wenn er ihn liest und mich sieht.

GASTON
Wie, Euer zukünftiger Schwiegervater hat Euch noch nie gesehen?

PINTO
Yes, yes, Don Gaston, I will marry a maiden.

GASTON
My soul, a maiden?

PINTO
The last of the line of Pacheco's in Madrid. Then we will call ourselves Fonseca y Pacheco!

AMBROSIO
(*in between brought wine, of which Pinto drinks much and quickly*)

GASTON
That sounds great—my best wishes, noble Don, for your engagement.

PINTO
Yes, you should wish me luck! Donna Clarissa is beautiful, rich and worthy of love—

GASTON
You lucky man!

PINTO
That is, I have not yet seen her, but my father said so. He ordered me to marry her.

GASTON
Ordered?

PINTO
Yes, the thing is settled between both fathers. They are childhood friends, and my father once arranged for my future father-in-law—(*He whispers something in Don Gaston's ear.*)

GASTON
(*astonished*) Ah!

PINTO
Yes, yes! And now I shall take his daughter Clarissa as my bride as a thank-you. Yes, yes, yes! You see, and now I travel to Madrid with this letter from my father. (*He pulls out a letter.*) Here it is. What could it contain?

GASTON
That I cannot say!

PINTO
Pity, pity!—Oh, the old Pacheco will be surprised when he reads it and sees me.

GASTON
What, your future father-in-law has not yet seen you?

PINTO
Nein, niemals, seht Ihr, das ist so lustig, daß es eine allgemeine Überraschung gibt: Ich kenne sie nicht, sie kennen mich nicht; sie kennt mich nicht, ich kenne sie nicht—Hahaha!

GASTON
Ja, das ist sehr lustig! Und Euer Herr Vater ist nicht mit auf die Brautfahrt gegangen?

PINTO
Ei, der liegt fest am Zipperlein—Hahaha, am Zipperlein!

GASTON
Hahaha, am Zipperlein!

PINTO
Wißt Ihr, Don Gaston, eigentlich ist mir's sehr unlieb, daß er nicht mit mir reisen kann—denn—versteht Ihr, versteht Ihr—ich weiß es nicht recht, wie man bei einer solchen Gelegenheit mir einer Dame umzugehen hat—wenn man so auf dem Lande lebt, da fehlt's gar sehr an Übung!

GASTON
Oh, es wird Euch ja nicht schwer fallen, das Richtige zu treffen, Don Pinto—bei Eurem ritterlichen Takt und feinem Anstande!—

PINTO
Hm hm, meint Ihr wirklich? Ich fürchte nur—

GASTON
Was fürchtet Ihr?

PINTO
Ich stoße an—

GASTON
Aber es ist doch gar nicht so schwer!

PINTO
Ja, die Übung fehlt, die Übung!

GASTON
Ei, für die soll schnell gesorgt sein! Ist's Euch recht, Don Pinto, so gehen wir die Werbung einmal durch.

PINTO
Wie Ihr wolltet?

GASTON
Natürlich, mit Freuden! Ich habe einige Erfahrung in solchen Dingen. Hier mein Diener Ambrosio soll die Braut sein—wenn Ihr's gestattet,—

AMBROSIO
Was—ich—die Braut?

PINTO
No, never, you see, it's so funny that there will a suprise all over: I don't know them, they don't know me; she doesn't know me, I don't know her—Hahaha!

GASTON
Yes, that's very funny. And your father will not be on the quest for the bride?

PINTO
Oh, he's laid up with gout—Hahaha, with gout!

GASTON
Hahaha, with gout!

PINTO
You know, Don Gaston, it is certainly very awkward for me that he cannot travel with me—because—you understand—I don't know the right way to treat a woman in such a situation as this—if you come from the country, you don't have much experience!

GASTON
Oh, it won't be a problem for you to do what's right, Don Pinto, with your noble tact and fine bearing!—

PINTO
Hm, hm, you really think so? I'm only afraid that—

GASTON
What frightens you?

PINTO
I make a mistake—

GASTON
But it's not so difficult!

PINTO
Yes, there is a lack of experience, experience!

GASTON
Oh, we will be seeing to that quickly! If it's all right with you, Don Pinto, we will run through the proposal now.

PINTO
Would you do that for me?

GASTON
Naturally, with pleasure! I have some experience in such matters. Here, my servant Ambrosio shall be the bride—if you permit—

AMBROSIO
What—me—the bride?

GASTON
(*leise*) Dummer Kerl, sperr Dich nicht, es gibt einen Hauptspaß! (*laut*) Gewiß, Du bist die Braut!

AMBROSIO
Nun gut denn—ich bin die Braut!

GASTON
Und ich, ich zeig' es Euch, wie Ihr's zu machen habt—Ihr werdet's mir leicht absehen!

PINTO
(*kindisch erfreut*) O, das ist herrlich, herrlich!

No. 6. Terzett

GASTON
Also frisch das Werk begonnen
Liebender Instruction!

PINTO
Ja, es sei das Werk begonnen
Liebender Instruction!

AMBROSIO
Was da wird, für Spaß ersonnen,
Darauf freue ich mich schon.

GASTON
(*zu Ambrosio*)
Setz' Dich dorthin, sittsam züchtig,
Und blick' g'rade vor Dich hin.

AMBROSIO
Nun, da sitz' ich, ist's so richtig?

GASTON
Gerade recht nach meinem Sinn!

PINTO
O, für mich welch ein Gewinn!

GASTON
(*zu Pinto*)
Nun komm' ich an Ihrer Stelle,
Trete über diese Schwelle
Flüchtig, schwebend, leise ein.

PINTO
Herrlich! Das scheint leicht zu sein!

GASTON
Nun probiren Sie's!

PINTO
Ich eile!
(*macht es tölpisch nach*)
Flüchtig—schwebend—

GASTON
Leiser, mild!

GASTON
(*softly*) Stupid idiot, don't hold back, it will be a good joke! (*loudly*) See, you will play the bride!

AMBROSIO
Now, good—I am the bride!

GASTON
And I, I'll show you what you have to do—you'll easily see from what I will do!

PINTO
(*childish joy*) Oh, this is great, just great!

No. 6. Terzett

GASTON
Quickly, let us begin the work
of instructing the lovers!

PINTO
Yes, the work of instructing lovers
is begun!

AMBROSIO
What it will be to contrive some fun!
I look forward to it already!

GASTON
(*to Ambrosio*)
Sit there, modestly, chastely,
and look straight ahead.

AMBROSIO
Now, I'm sitting, it is correct?

GASTON
Exactly as I said!

PINTO
Oh, what a good thing for me!

GASTON
(*to Pinto*)
Now, I come in your place,
step over the threshold,
quickly, delicately, lightly.

PINTO
Great! That looks easy to do!

GASTON
Now you try it!

PINTO
I hurry!
(*does so awkwardly*)
Quickly—delicately—

GASTON
More softly, milder!

PINTO (*macht es nochmals*) Ist's so recht? **GASTON** (*nickt beifällig*) Noch eine Weile Steh'n Sie dann, als ob das Bild Hoher Schönheit Sie betäube, Wonnezitternd ganz am Leibe! (*Stellung*) **PINTO** Ja, das will ich herrlich machen! (*ahmt es nach*) **GASTON** Ganz vortrefflich geh'n die Sachen! **PINTO** Gelt, das kann ich herrlich machen! **AMBROSIO** Halten kann ich kaum das Lachen! **GASTON** Nun gestürzet zu den Füßen Der Geliebten, Holden, Süßen! Dann ergreifen Sie die Hand, Heiß von Liebesgluth entbrannt! (*thut es*) **PINTO** Ach, wie ritterlich galant! Wohl, ich stürze hin und küsse! **AMBROSIO** Sie zertrampeln mir die Füße! **GASTON** Sitzen bleiben, Fräulein Braut! Noch einmal! **PINTO** Nun aufgeschaut! (*Er macht es noch einmal.*) **GASTON** Jetzo springt sie auf erschrocken!— (*zu Ambrosio*) Rede nur, kennst ja die Brocken! **AMBROSIO** Welche Kühnheit! **GASTON** Oh, ich kann Diesem Reiz nicht widerstehen! Hier zu Ihren Füßen flehen—	**PINTO** (*tries it again*) Is this right? **GASTON** (*nods complimentarily*) And for a while you stand as though the image of great beauty overcame you, shuddering with joy through your entire body. (*posing*) **PINTO** Yes, I will do it nobly! (*imitates it*) **GASTON** Things are going most spendidly! **PINTO** You see, I can do it right! **AMBROSIO** I can hardly keep from laughing! **GASTON** Now fall to the feet of the beloved, the dear one, the sweet one! Then take her by the hand, warmed by the passion of love. (*He does it.*) **PINTO** Oh, how noble, how gallant! Well, I fall down and kiss! **AMBROSIO** You're stepping on my feet! **GASTON** Remain sitting, Miss Bride! Once more! **PINTO** Now look up! (*He does it yet again.*) **GASTON** Now she jumps up frightened— (*to Ambrosio*) Only speak, you know the words! **AMBROSIO** What courage! **GASTON** Oh, I cannot resist these charms. Here at your feet, I beseech you—

AMBROSIO Steh'n Sie auf, Sie loser Mann!	**AMBROSIO** Get up, you teasing man!
PINTO Soll mich gleich der Teufel holen Mache ich mich auf die Sohlen Eh' ich einen Schmatz gewann!	**PINTO** The devil take me! I shall run away before I win a kiss!
GASTON Eher nicht, als bis ich weiß, Ob Verzeihung ich gewann.	**GASTON** Not until I know whether I won pardon.
AMBROSIO (*mit weiblicher Stimme*) Nun, man ist doch nicht von Eis—! (*reicht Gaston die Hand zum Kusse; Gaston steht auf.*)	**AMBROSIO** (*in falsetto*) Now, one is not made of ice—! (*extends the hand for Gaston to kiss; Gaston stands up.*)
PINTO Schön! Vortrefflich! Will's probiren! (*wirft sich Ambrosio zu Füßen*)	**PINTO** Beautiful! Splendid! I want to try it! (*throws himself at Ambrosio's feet*)
AMBROSIO Welche Kühnheit!	**AMBROSIO** What courage!
PINTO Sapperlot, Ihr seid zum Verstand verlieren! Vor Entzücken bin ich todt!	**PINTO** The dickens, you make me lose my reason! I die with ecstasy!
AMBROSIO (*mit weiblicher Stimme*) Steh'n Sie auf, Sie loser Mann!	**AMBROSIO** (*in falsetto*) Stand up, teasing man!
PINTO Soll mich gleich der Teufel holen, Mache ich mich auf die Sohlen Eh' ich einen Schmatz gewann!	**PINTO** The devil take me, I shall run away before I win a kiss.
GASTON Nein, noch nicht! Kommt später d'ran! (*Pinto steht auf.*) Jetzo weiter! "Holde Schöne, Bin ich von dem Glück erlesen, Daß Dein himmlischsüßes Wesen All' mein Leben kröne?"	**GASTON** No, not yet! That comes later! (*Pinto stands.*) Now further! "Lovely Beauty, am I so fortunate that your heavenly being should crown all my life?"
PINTO Ach, das klingt doch gar zu herrlich— Aber—o, das lern' ich schwerlich!	**PINTO** Ah, that sounds so noble— but—oh, I learn with difficulty!
GASTON Nur versucht, es wird schon geh'n!	**GASTON** Now try, it will go well!
PINTO Holde Schöne, die sehr schön, Ich bin toll ganz vor Entzücken, Daß Sie zuckersüßes Wesen Mich zu Ihren Mann erlesen Und mich krönen—	**PINTO** Lovely beauty, who is very beautiful, I am crazy with rapture that you, sugar-sweet creature, chose me as your husband and shall crown—

GASTON Blicken Sie in's Aug' ihr glühend heiß!	**GASTON** Look into her eyes with warm passion!
PINTO (*thut es*)	**PINTO** (*does so*)
GASTON Wie er das zu machen weiß! Und nun schlingen Sie den Arm Um den Leib ihr—so, ganz leise.	**GASTON** How he knows what to do! And now put your arm around her body—so lightly.
AMBROSIO (*mit Mädchenstimme*) Ach, wie wird mir doch so warm!	**AMBROSIO** (*in falsetto*) Oh, how this warms me!
GASTON Und nun rasch die süße Speise Von den Lippen sich genascht, Die allein der Liebe eigen.	**GASTON** And now quickly snatch the sweet food from her lips, which love alone owns.
AMBROSIO (*mit natürlicher Stimme*) Soll ich dann bereit mich zeigen?	**AMBROSIO** (*in normal voice*) Should I then show myself to be ready?
GASTON Freilich, freilich!	**GASTON** Naturally, naturally!
PINTO Frisch, d'rauf los! (*Er giebt Ambrosio einen tüchtigen Kuß, dieser sinkt in seine Arme.*)	**PINTO** Let's go! (*He gives a powerful kiss to Ambrosio, who sinks in his arms.*)
AMBROSIO Ach, der Liebe Macht ist groß!	**AMBROSIO** Oh, the power of love is great!
GASTON Bravo, bravo, so wird's gehen! Herrlich werden Sie's verstehen, Wie nach allerneustem Schnitt Vor die Braut der Bräut'gam tritt!	**GASTON** Bravo, bravo! That will be fine! You'll understand how wonderful it is, how in the latest fashion, the groom approaches the bride!
PINTO Bravo, bravo, so wird's gehen! Kinderleicht ist's zu verstehen, Wie nach allerneustem Schnitt Vor die Braut der Bräut'gam tritt!	**PINTO** Bravo, bravo! So it goes! It is child's play to understand how of the latest fashion, the groom approaches the bride!
AMBROSIO Bravo, bravo, ich muß gestehen, Besser kann es gar nicht gehen! Wenn er vor die Braut so tritt, Nimmt er ihr die Füße mit!	**AMBROSIO** Bravo, bravo! I must confess, that it cannot go better! If he stands so before the bride, he'll stomp on her feet!
PINTO (*zu Gaston*) Schönen Dank!	**PINTO** (*to Gaston*) Many thanks!
GASTON Gar nicht nöthig!	**GASTON** It's really nothing!

PINTO
(*zu Ambrosio*)
Große Schuld—

AMBROSIO
Gern' erbötig!

PINTO
So die Blicke?

GASTON
Zum Ergeben!

PINTO
(*zu Ambrosio*)
Süße Schöne!

AMBROSIO
(*mit Mädchenstimme*)
Du mein Leben!

ALLE DREI
Ganz vortrefflich, wunderschön,
Herrlich, herrlich wird das geh'n.

Scene 6

Die Vorigen. Inez und die Dienstleute bringen Speisen und Getränke. Sie decken den Tisch für Gaston und Pinto.

DIALOG
PINTO
Ha, endlich, endlich das Essen! Mein Himmel, dieser Hunger, dieser Hunger!

INEZ
(*macht Gaston und Pinto einen Knix*) Wäre es den edlen Herrn gefällig?

PINTO
Hahah—Du bist gefällig, mein Kind—Hahaha! (*setzt sich sofort und fängt an zu essen*)

GASTON
Ausgezeichnetes Wortspiel—Hahaha!

AMBROSIO
Hahaha!

GASTON
Nun—laß sehen, Inez, was Eure Wirtschaft leistet—

PINTO
(*mit vollen Backen*) Seht lieber zu, was ich nun leisten werde—dieser Hunger!

GASTON
Du wirst uns doch Deine Gesellschaft bei Tische gönnen?

PINTO
(*to Ambrosio*)
A great debt—

AMBROSIO
Happy to help!

PINTO
These looks?

GASTON
Looks to conquer!

PINTO
(*to Ambrosio*)
Sweet beauty!

AMBROSIO
(*in falsetto*)
You are my life!

ALL THREE
Most splendidly, wonderfully,
great, it will go well.

Scene 6

As before. Inez and the servers bring food and drink. They set the table for Gaston and Pinto.

DIALOGUE
PINTO
Ha! At last, at last the food! My heavens, this hunger, this hunger!

INEZ
(*curtsies to Gaston and Pinto*) Would the gentlemen like to eat?

PINTO
Hahah—you are pleasing, my child—Hahaha! (*sits down directly and begins to eat*)

GASTON
Extraodinary wordplay—Hahaha!

AMBROSIO
Hahaha!

GASTON
Now—let us see, Inez, what your hospitality achieves—

PINTO
(*with a full mouth*) Rather, let's see what I now will achieve—this hunger!

GASTON
Would you grant us your company at the table?

INEZ
(*auf Pinto blickend*) Es ist gar Vielerlei im Haus zu thun!

GASTON
Ihr gestattet doch, Don Pinto, daß unsere liebenswürdige Wirthtochter sich zu uns setzt?

PINTO
Meinetwegen, meinetwegen! Es scheint ja genug zu essen da zu sein.

GASTON
Das mein' ich auch—d'rum wenn's beliebt, holde Inez! (*Inez setzt sich.*) Nun wird das Mahl uns doppelt munden!

PINTO
Ei, warum denn?

GASTON
Ein schönes Mädchen bei Tisch ist die beste Labung für Herz und Auge—

PINTO
Das merk' ich mir: Ein schönes Mädchen ist die beste Speise—Hahaha!

GASTON
Bravo, bravo, Don Pinto! Ihr lernt schnell!

No. 7. Finale

INEZ
Auf das Wohlergeh'n der Gäste!
(*Sie stößt mit Gaston an.*)

GASTON
Schön bedankt!

INEZ
(*wendet sich an Pinto*)

PINTO
(*kauend, weist sie ab*)
Ist schon gut!

GASTON
Du bewirthest uns auf's Beste!

INEZ
Gut wird, was man gerne thut!

GASTON
Auf das Wohl der schönen Inez!

INEZ
Schön bedankt!

PINTO
Ist schon gut!

INEZ
(*looking at Pinto*) There is much in the house to be done!

GASTON
Do you allow, Don Pinto, that our kind innkeeper's daughter sits with us?

PINTO
For all I care, for all I care! There seems really enough to eat.

GASTON
I think so, too—so as you please, dear Inez! (*Inez seats herself.*) Now will the meal delight us double!

PINTO
Oh, why then?

GASTON
A beautiful maiden at the table is the best refreshment for heart and eyes—

PINTO
I said that to myself: A beautiful maiden is the best food—Hahaha!

GASTON
Bravo, bravo, Don Pinto! You learn quickly!

No. 7. Finale

INEZ
To the health of the guests!
(*She toasts with Gaston.*)

GASTON
Many thanks!

INEZ
(*turns to Pinto*)

PINTO
(*chewing, turns away from her*)
It's very good!

GASTON
You serve us the best!

INEZ
It's good, what one does well!

GASTON
To the health of the beautiful Inez!

INEZ
Many thanks!

PINTO
It's very good!

GASTON
(*kauend*)
Welche öde Menschenseele!

INEZ
(*zu Gaston*)
Die kommt nicht so leicht in Gluth.

GASTON
(*aufspringend, bei Seite*)
Nein, das werd' ich nimmer leiden,
Daß ein solches Kalbsgesicht
Zum Altare sollt' geleiten
Einen Engel hold und licht.

PINTO
Ja, das Weinchen läßt sich trinken,
Welche Würze, welche Macht!
Und der Alte zahlt die Schulden,
Die das Söhnchen heute macht!

INEZ
Gott bewahr' vor solchem Freier
Mich mein ganzes Leben lang!
Am Altar—zur Hochzeitsfeier—
Ach, da wird mir angst und bang!

AMBROSIO
Solch ein Tölpel zieht auf Freite
Nach der Schönsten Donna aus!
Geb' der Teufel Ihm's Geleite!
Hoffentlich wird Nichts daraus!

GASTON
(*Der einen Entschluß gefaßt, nachdem er Ambrosio eine leise Weisung gegeben.*)
Darum, als ein echter Ritter,
Rett' ich die bedrängte Maid.

PINTO
Dieses Hähnchen schmeckt nicht bitter—
Und das Weinchen thut kein Leid.

INEZ
Lieber hinter'm Klostergitter,
Als solch einen Mann gefreit!

GASTON
(*tritt an die Tafel zurück, höchst heiter*)
Schenkt ein, schenkt ein,
Heut' soll der Wein
In vollen Strömen fließen!
(*zu den Leuten*)
Sollt Alle mitgenießen,
Alle herbei,
Trinket nun frei!
(*Ambrosio schenkt den Dienstleuten Wein ein.*)

INEZ
Was fällt ihnen ein?

GASTON
(*chewing*)
What a boring soul!

INEZ
(*to Gaston*)
It doesn't glow easily.

GASTON
(*jumping up, to the side*)
No, I will never allow,
that such a calf's face
should take to the altar
an angel dear and light.

PINTO
Yes, that's a nice, drinkable wine,
such bouquet, such power!
And the father pays the debt,
that the son makes today!

INEZ
God keep me from such a suitor
my entire life long!
At the altar—for the wedding—
ah, it gives me fear and worry!

AMBROSIO
Such an oaf goes to court
the most beautiful lady!
The devil take him!
I hope that nothing will come of it!

GASTON
(*He makes a decision, after which he gives Ambrosio a short direction.*)
Thus, as a true knight,
I will save a bothered maiden.

PINTO
This chicken doesn't taste bitter—
and the wine isn't bad.

INEZ
It's better to hide in a convent,
than to marry such a husband!

GASTON
(*steps back to the table, in greatest joy*)
Pour, pour,
today the wine should
flow in full streams!
(*to the people*)
All should enjoy,
all here,
drink on the house!
(*Ambrosio pours wine for the servers.*)

INEZ
What are you doing,

Laden Alle ein!

PINTO
Er muß ein Narr wohl sein!
Trink' lieber für mich allein!

AMBROSIO
Er muß ein Narr wohl sein:
Hat nichts im Sack
Und läd't And're ein!

CHOR
Es lebe der Wein, der Wein!

GASTON
Getrunken, Herr Ritter, getrunken—
Dann springet der geistige Funken
Aus Seele, aus Hirn und Gemüth!

PINTO
(*lallend*)
Ich habe schon tüchtig geladen—
Und mehr noch könnte mir schaden,
Es ist mir, wie wenn doppelt man sieht!

GASTON
(*zu Inez*)
Es lebe die Schönheit, die Liebe!

CHOR
Sie leben!

PINTO
Mir wird vor den Augen ganz trübe!

INEZ
(*zu den Herren*)
Es lebe die Weisheit, die Stärke!

PINTO
Sie le—, es ist mir—ich merke—

GASTON
Don Pinto, die Reih' ist an Ihnen!

AMBROSIO
(*parodirend*)
Ist schon gut, ist schon gut!

PINTO
Ich kann Euch damit nicht dienen!

INEZ
(*neckend zu Pinto*)
Was wird Ihr Herr Vater denn sagen?

PINTO
(*erschreckend*)
Ja so—der Papa! Nun, es lebe—der Magen!
(*alle lachen*)

---

inviting everyone?

PINTO
He must be a real fool!
I'd rather drink by myself!

AMBROSIO
He must be a real fool:
Nothing in his pocket
and he invites everyone!

CHORUS
Long live the wine, the wine!

GASTON
Drink, sir knight, drink—
then the intellectual spark jumps forth
from the soul, from the mind and heart!

PINTO
(*humming*)
I'm already powerfully loaded—
and more could do me harm.
It seems as though I'm seeing double!

GASTON
(*to Inez*)
Long live beauty, love!

CHORUS
May they live!

PINTO
Everything before my eyes blurs!

INEZ
(*to the men*)
Long live wisdom, strength!

PINTO
Long live—it seems that—I note—

GASTON
Don Pinto, it's your turn!

AMBROSIO
(*in parody*)
It's very good, it's very good!

PINTO
I cannot serve you with that!

INEZ
(*teasing Pinto*)
What would your father say?

PINTO
(*shocked*)
Oh, yes—Papa!—Now, long live—my stomach!
(*all laugh*)

GASTON
Der Geber so herrlicher Freuden
Zieht stets sich zurück so bescheiden:
Heut' sei ihm ein Vivat gebracht!

PINTO
(*mit zitternder Stimme*)
Ein Vivat—ja, ja—gute Nacht!
(*will einschlafen*)

GASTON
(*ihn rüttelnd*)
Fein munter und lustig geblieben!

AMBROSIO
(*zu Pinto*)
Gute Nacht, gute Nacht!

PINTO
(*aufwachend*)
Ja—munter—
(*Er schläft ein.*)

GASTON
(*zu Pinto, ihn rüttelnd, sodaß dieser auffährt*)
Frisch auf! Was wir lieben!

CHOR
Was wir lieben, was wir lieben!

PINTO
Was wir—über
(*schläft wieder ein*)

CHOR
Was wir lieben, was wir lieben!
Was uns hold und treu geblieben!
Der da schickt sich nicht zum Lieben,
Nein, nein, nein, nein!

GASTON
(*Der sich unterdessen an Pinto gemacht und ihm den Brief aus dem Wams gezogen.*)
Diesen Brief hier sich zu rauben,
Ist kein Diebstahl sollt' ich glauben:
Denn, was auch Papa geschrieben,
Dieser schickt sich nicht zum Lieben.
(*zum Chor*)
Seht, da ist er eingeschlafen,
Tragt ihn in des Bettes Hafen,
Bis ihm nach des Rausches Nacht
Heller Morgen wieder lacht!

CHOR
Steif und fest schlief er hier ein!
Ei, der mag betrunken sein!
[Munter, munter, munter!]

GASTON
The giver of such wonderful joys
always withdraws with such modesty:
Today we salute him with "vivat"!

PINTO
(*with a stuttering voice*)
A "vivat"—yes, yes—good night!
(*wants to sleep*)

GASTON
(*shaking him*)
Stay awake and remain joyful!

AMBROSIO
(*to Pinto*)
Good night, good night!

PINTO
(*waking up*)
Yes, awake!—
(*He falls asleep.*)

GASTON
(*to Pinto, shaking him, so that he gets up*)
Awake! To what we love!

CHORUS
What we love, what we love!

PINTO
What we—over
(*falls back asleep*)

CHORUS
What we love, what we love!
What we hold dear and true!
This one is not made for love,
No, no, no, no!

GASTON
(*He reaches under Pinto and pulls the letter out of his jacket.*)

To steal this letter here,
I believe is no theft:
For, whatever Papa wrote,
this one is not made for love.
(*to the Chorus*)
See, there he is asleep,
carry him to the safety of his bed,
so that after this drunken night,
a bright morning may smile on him!

CHORUS
Stiff and soundly he sleeps!
Oh, he may be drunken!
[Awake, awake, awake!]

GASTON
Laßt ihn schlafen, laßt ihn schlafen,
(*für sich*)
Seinen Brief hab' ich geborgen,
Noch zur Stunde reis' ich fort!
(*zum Chor*)
In die Kammer tragt ihn dort!
Dort soll er zur Ruhe geh'n,
Wissen nicht, wie ihm gescheh'n.
Ruhig, ruhig, stille, still!

CHOR
Aber tragt ihn leis' und sacht,
Daß der Schläfer nicht erwacht!
Dort soll er zur Ruhe geh'n.
Morgen mag er selber seh'n,
Ob er weiter reisen will.
Darum leise, leise, sacht,
Ruhig, ruhig, stille, still!
Freunde tragt ihn leis' und sacht
Daß der Schläfer nicht erwacht!
Dort soll er zur Ruhe geh'n,
Wissen nicht wie ihm gescheh'n!
(*Sie tragen Pinto durch die Thüre in das Innere des Hauses.*)

(*Ende des ersten Aufzuges*)

Zweiter Aufzug

(*Saal im Palaste Don Pantaleone's de Pacheco zu Madrid. An den Wänden Ahnenbilder.*)

Scene 1

Die Dienerschaft Don Pantaleone's gruppenweise im Gespräch.

No. 8. Introduction
CHOR
Wißt Ihr nicht, was wir hier sollen?
Weiß es Keiner?—Du nicht? Nein!
Was mag nur der Herr heut' wollen,
Was doch hier die Absicht sein?
In den Ahnensaal entboten
Hat er Alle uns hierher,
Um vor seinen großen Todten,
Zu verkünden neue Mähr'!
Wicht'ges kann doch nur bedeuten,
Was man sagt vor solchen Leuten!
(*Sie verbeugen sich vor den Bildern.*)
Doch er kommt, seid Alle still,
Bald erfahrt Ihr, was er will!
Höret was er sagen will: still!

GASTON
Let him sleep, let him sleep,
(*to himself*)
I am guarding his letter,
yet I leave in an hour!
(*to the Chorus*)
Carry him to the room there!
There he should get some rest,
he doesn't know what happened.
Peace, peace, calm, calm!

CHORUS
But carry him lightly and gently,
so that the sleeper doesn't awaken!
There he should get some rest.
Tomorrow may he see for himself,
whether he will travel further.
Thus, lightly, lightly, gently,
peace, peace, calm, calm!
Friends, carry him lightly and gently,
so that the sleeper doesn't awaken!
There he should get some rest,
he doesn't know what happened!
(*They carry Pinto through the door, inside, into the house.*)

(*end of the first act*)

Act Two

(*A hall in the palace of Don Pantaleone de Pacheco in Madrid. On the walls are portraits of his ancestors.*)

Scene 1

The servants of Don Pantaleone group together in conversation.

No. 8. Introduction
CHORUS
Do you know what we're doing here?
No one knows?—Not you? No!
I wonder what the master may want today,
what the purpose here may be?
In the ancestral hall he called us
all together to announce new tidings
in front of his great forebears!
It can only mean something
important, whatever you say
in front of such people!
(*They bow before the portraits.*)
Here he comes, all be still,
soon you will find out what he wants!
Listen to what he will say: Quiet!

Scene 2

Vorige. Clarissa und Laura (treten ein).

LAURA
Nur herein, Gebieterin!

CLARISSA
Ach, mich faßt ein banges Ahnen!

LAURA
Fester Muth und froher Sinn
Werden unsere Wege bahnen!

CLARISSA
Seine Reden, seine Blicke—
Dunkel spricht er mir von Glücke—
Ach, ich kenne doch nur eins
Und von diesem ferne keins.

LAURA
Trotz der Reden, trotz der Blicke
Zweifelt nicht an Eurem Glücke.
Ist der Grund fest des Vereins,
Steht auch fest der Bau des Seins.

CHOR, CLARISSA, LAURA
Darum wollen wir erwarten,
Was der alte Herr wird karten,
Bald wird nun der Neugier Lohn,
Denn seht hin, da naht er schon!
Aber seht, da naht er schon, seht!

Scene 3

Vorige. Don Pantaleone (festlich gekleidet).

PANTALEONE
Berufen hab' ich Dich hierher, mein Kind,
Und Euch als Zeugen, liebe Vielgetreue,
Daß Ihr vernehmt, was wir gesonnen sind
Zu thun, und Jeder sich darob erfreue!

CHOR
Wir sind dazu bereit,
Im Voraus schon erfreut.

PANTALEONE
Don Roiz de Pacheco altem Stamme
Entsproßt nur eine einz'ge Blüte noch:
Da seht Ihr sie!
(deutet auf Clarissa)
Da ist es nöthig doch
Daß man das Feuer wiederum entflamme!

CHOR
Das scheint uns ganz gerecht;
Doch sprecht nur weiter, sprecht!

PANTALEONE
(zu Clarissa)
D'rum hab' ich Dir 'nen Bräutigam erlesen,

Scene 2

As before. Clarissa and Laura (enter).

LAURA
Come in, my mistress!

CLARISSA
Ah, a strange foreboding comes over me!

LAURA
Solid courage and a happy mind
will lead us on our way!

CLARISSA
His speech, his look—
he spoke darkly to me of happiness—
ah, I know only one joy,
and far away from him—none.

LAURA
Despite the speech, despite the looks
don't doubt your happiness.
If the basis of your union is strong,
the building stands firm.

CHORUS, CLARISSA, LAURA
Thus, we want to await,
what the old master will plan,
soon our curiosity will be satisfied,
look, here he comes!
But see, he draws near!

Scene 3

As before. Don Pantaleone (festively dressed).

PANTALEONE
I've called you here, my child,
and you as witness, dear faithful,
that you will hear what we are prepared to do,
and so that everyone may rejoice!

CHORUS
We are ready for it,
in advance we already rejoice.

PANTALEONE
From the old line of Don Roiz de Pacheco,
there springs only one blossom:
You see her there!
(indicates Clarissa)
Therefore we need to make
the fire burn again!

CHORUS
That seems to us entirely fair;
yet say more, speak!

PANTALEONE
(to Clarissa)
Thus, I have chosen a bridegroom for you,

Mein Kind, ja, ja, Clarissa, Du bist Braut.
Und ein Fonseca, dessen Vater einst gewesen
Ein Retter mir, Don Pinto, wird Dir angetraut!

CLARISSA
(*für sich*)
Don Pinto, Vater—? Nein!

LAURA
(*für sich*)
Da schlägt der Blitz schon ein!

CHOR
Das nenn' ich Vater sein,
Welch' glücklicher Verein!

PANTALEONE
Und heute schon, so zeigt des Briefes Datum,
Trifft er hier ein und fordert Deine Hand.
D'rum preist mit mir das wunderbare Fatum,
Das uns Don Pinto hierher hergesandt.

CHOR
Welche Wonne, welch' Entzücken!
Ja, bald strahlet aus den Blicken
Der Verlobten sel'ge Lust.
Hoher Herr wir wünschen Segen!
Holde Braut, Euch strömt entgegen
Schon der Quell der reinsten Lust.

LAURA
Wie beklommen ist das arme Herz
Soll den Vater sie bewegen
Wird in ihm sich Mitleid regen
Dass nicht sterbe jede Lust?

CLARISSA UND LAURA
Gott, auf welche Schicksalstücken
Muß ich/sie in die Zukunft blicken,
Wie beklommen ist die Brust!
Soll den Vater ich/sie bewegen,
Werd'/Wird sein Mitleid ich/sie erregen
Daß nicht sterbe jede Lust?

PANTALEONE
Jetzt entfernt Euch, zuzuschicken,
Was das Fest vermag zu schmücken,
Fort, hinweg ohn' Zeitverlust!
Alles soll die Hände regen,
Doch auch dann sich weidlich pflegen:
Nach der Arbeit folgt die Lust.

[DIALOG]
LAURA
Habt nur Muth, es wird noch glücken! (*zu Pantaleone*) Seht doch nur aus ihren Blicken Leuchtet frohe Liebeslust! (*zu Clarissa*) Fräulein, auf den schlimmsten Wegen Kommt der beste Rath entgegen. (*zu Pantaleone*) Daß ich das erleben mußt'! (*Dienerschaft und Don Pantaleone ab.*)

---

my child, yes, yes, Clarissa, you are a bride.
And a Fonseca, whose father once was
a savior to me, Don Pinto, will be betrothed to you.

CLARISSA
(*to herself*)
Don Pinto, father? No!

LAURA
(*to herself*)
Lightning struck there!

CHORUS
I will call that a father,
what a happy union!

PANTALEONE
And already today, as shown in the date of the letter,
he will arrive here and ask your hand.
Thus, praise with me the wonderful fate,
that sent Don Pinto to us!

CHORUS
What bliss, what delight!
Yes, soon their eyes will sparkle
with the holy joy of lovers.
Great Lord, we wish you blessings!
Dear bride, to you already
the source of pure happiness is beckoning.

LAURA
How uneasy is the poor heart
should she move the father,
will compassion rule him,
so that joy will not die?

CLARISSA AND LAURA
God, what turns of fate
must I/she see in the future,
how uneasy is the breast!
Should I/she move the father,
will I/she incite his compassion
so that joy will not die?

PANTALEONE
Now depart, to send
what may decorate the feast,
away, away without delay!
All should occupy their hands
yet then also relax thoroughly:
After work comes enjoyment.

[DIALOGUE]
LAURA
Just have courage, it will turn out well! (*to Pantaleone*) See, her eyes are sparkling with the joy of love! (*to Clarissa*) Dear, on the worst paths the best counsel will come to you. (*to Pantaleone*) I must live to see that! (*Servants and Don Pantaleone leave.*)

Scene 4

Clarissa, Laura

DIALOG

CLARISSA
Laura! Laura! Hast Du's vernommen! Ich Unglückselige!

LAURA
Muth, Muht, Herrin!—

CLARISSA
Muth in dieser verzweifelten Lage!

LAURA
Herrin, habt Ihr nie gedacht, daß dieser Augenblick kommen werde?

CLARISSA
Gewiß! So oft mein Vater auf meine Verheiratung anspielte, gab es mir einen Stich in's Herz und ich sann auf ein Mittel, dem Schicksal, das mir droht, zu entrinnen—denn Laura, nur Gomez soll mein Gatte werden, sonst Keiner, das schwöre ich!

LAURA
Oh Herrin, wenn Ihr Euer selbst so sicher sid, so muß es ja gelingen, diesem Don Pinto zu entgehen!

CLARISSA
Ach ich habe vergebens nachgesonnen!

LAURA
Die Hauptsache ist, daß Ihr Don Gomez treu und unwandelbar liebt, und daß er Euch wieder liebt.

CLARISSA
Eher ließe er sein Leben, als seine Liebe!

LAURA
Ei seht, auf wie festem Grunde Ihr dann steht und wie glücklich Ihr darüber sein solltet, statt zu verzagen.

CLARISSA
Ach Laura!

NO. 9. ARIETTE

LAURA
"Höchste Lust ist treues Lieben!"
Ruft es rings mit tausend Stimmen.
In den Sternen siehst Du's flimmern:
"Höchste Lust ist treues Lieben!"
In den Lüften rauscht's, den Linden,
Alle Blumen wollen's künden,
An dem Himmel steht's geschrieben:
"Höchste Lust ist treues Lieben!"

Ja, dort steht's geschrieben!
D'rum Gebieterin,
Weg den trüben Sinn,

Scene 4

Clarissa, Laura

DIALOGUE

CLARISSA
Laura! Laura! Have you heard! I am unfortunate!

LAURA
Courage, courage, mistress!—

CLARISSA
Courage in these desperate circumstances!

LAURA
Mistress, haven't you thought that this moment would come?

CLARISSA
Certainly! Whenever father hinted at marriage it gave me a pain in the heart and I conceived of a means to evade the fate that was threatening me—because, Laura, only Gomez shall be my husband, no one else, that I swear to you!

LAURA
Oh, mistress, if you are so sure of yourself, then you must succeed in escaping this Don Pinto!

CLARISSA
Ah, I have reflected in vain!

LAURA
The main thing is that you love Don Gomez truly and unswervingly, and that he loves you in return.

CLARISSA
He would sooner lose his life than his love!

LAURA
Oh, see, then you stand on solid ground. How happy you should then be about it, instead of despairing.

CLARISSA
Ah, Laura!

NO. 9. ARIETTA

LAURA
"The highest joy is true love!"
Shout it with a thousand voices.
In the stars you see it glimmer:
"The highest joy is true love!"
In the breezes, it resounds in the linden trees,
all the flowers announce it,
it's written in heaven:
"The highest joy is true love!"

Yes, there it's written!
Thus, my lady,
away with the gloomy mind,

Sorgen weg, Thränen weg,	cares away, tears away,
Bald lacht der Sonne Blick!	soon the sun will be smiling!
Froh vollendet sich's	It will resolve happily,
Fröhlich endet sich's!	everything will end joyfully!
Bald kehrt das Glück	Soon happiness
Wieder zurück	comes back
In Euer Herz!	into your heart!
"Reinstes Glück ist treues Lieben!"	"The purest joy is true love!"
Lächelt Dir's im Morgenstrahle,	Thus it smiles at you in the morning light,
Blinkt Dir's aus der vollen Schale.	it winks at you from full cups.
"Reinstes Glück ist treues Lieben!"	"The purest joy is true love!"
Sprudelnd ruft es aus der Quelle	Bubbling it calls from the spring,
Schimmernd gleitet's auf der Welle,	shimmering it glides on the wave,
Grünend sproßt's aus allen Trieben:	budding it sprouts off all branches:
"Reinstes Glück ist treues Lieben!"	"The purest happiness is true love!"
D'rum Gebieterin	Thus, my lady,
Weg den trüben Sinn,	away with the gloomy mind,
Sorgen weg, Thränen weg,	cares away, tears away,
Bald lacht der Sonne Blick!	soon the sun will be smiling!
Froh vollendet sich's	There will be a happy ending,
Fröhlich endet sich's!	a joyful conclusion!
Bald kehrt das Glück	Soon happiness
Wieder zurück	comes back
In Euer Herz!	into your heart!

Dialog / Dialogue

CLARISSA

Dein leichter Sinn kann wirklich an eine glückliche Wendung glauben?

Does your carefree disposition permit you to believe in a happy ending?

LAURA

Nicht mein leichter Sinn, sondern meine feste Zuversicht.

Not my happy disposition, but rather my firm confidence.

CLARISSA

Aber welchen Weg einschlagen?

But which path do you suggest?

LAURA

Habt Ihr je Eurem Vater von Don Gomez gesprochen, von seiner edlen Gesinnung, seinem Geist, von seiner Familie—seinem Vermögen?

Have you ever spoken to your father about Don Gomez, of his noble mind, his intelligence, of his family—his fortune?

CLARISSA

Wohl tat ich es. Aber Gomez ihm vorstellen, durfte ich ja nicht, da er sich seines unseligen Duells wegen verborgen halten muß! Mein Vater kennt ihn nicht und hat ihn nie gesehen—oh, wenn er ihn kennte!

I've already done it. But I was not able to introduce Gomez to him, since Gomez had to stay in hiding because of his unfortunate duel! My father doesn't know him and has never seen him—oh, if only he knew him!

LAURA

Vielleicht ginge er doch mal von seiner Idee ab!

Maybe then he would give up his idea!

CLARISSA

Nein, nein, es ist zu spät! Besinne Dich nur, wie er von diesen Fonsecas schwärmt, wie er sie liebt, und nun sollte er im Augenblicke vor der Erfüllung seines Lieblingswunsches davon abstehen, einen Fonseca seinen Schwiegersohn zu nennen? Nimmermehr!

No, no, it is too late! Only consider how he adores these Fonsecas, how he loves them, and now, should he shortly before the fulfillment of his dearest wish, refuse to take a Fonseca as his son-in-law? Never!

LAURA
Und was verbindet ihn dem alten Fonseca so fest?

CLARISSA
Fonseca hat meinem Vater einst einen großen Dienst erwiesen!

LAURA
So? Aber sagt mir doch, was dann wohl den alten Fonseca bewegen mag, auf diese Heirat einzugehen?

CLARISSA
Sind die Fonsecas nicht verarmt und bin ich nicht eine reiche Erbin?

LAURA
O Himmel, Ihr habt Recht! Nein, aber Ihr sollt nicht verkauft werden! Ich eile zu Don Gomez—er muß Rat schaffen.—

CLARISSA
Wie, zu Gomez—was willst Du wagen?

LAURA
Alles, Herrin und auch er wird alles für Euch wagen! Also Mut, Mut! Wir finden einen Ausweg! (*ab*)

Scene 5.

Clarissa (allein)

No. 10. Recitativ

Ach, wenn dies Du doch vermöchtest!
Wenn Du mir durch Deinen Scherz
Hoffnung trügst in's bange Herz
Und den Schmerz zum Schweigen brächtest!
Aber ach, ich fürchte nur zu sehr,
Lebensfreude blüht für mich nicht mehr!

Arie

Wonnesüßes Hoffnungsträumen
Wie durchströmest Du mein Herz!
Willst die Wolken rosig säumen
Ruhe geben meinem Schmerz,
Selig möcht' ich weiter träumen,
Schwelgen in der holden Lust,
Die mir blüht in deinen Schäumen—
Doch das Herz zersprengt die Brust.
Ach wie so bange
Ist dein Klopfen,
Auf die Wange
Rinnen Tropfen
Heißer Thränen!
Ach all' mein Sehnen
Kennt nur einen Gegenstand!

Nie verstand ich,
Nie empfand ich
Solch' Entzücken,

LAURA
And what ties him so tightly to the old Fonseca?

CLARISSA
Fonseca once rendered my father a great service!

LAURA
So? Yet tell me, what then moved old Fonseca to think about this marriage?

CLARISSA
Aren't the Fonsecas impoverished and am I not a rich heiress?

LAURA
Oh heavens, you are right! But no, you shall not be sold! I will rush to Don Gomez—he must find an alternative.—

CLARISSA
How, to Gomez—what are you daring to do?

LAURA
All, mistress, and he, too, will dare everything for you! Therefore, courage, courage! We will find a way out! (*leaves*)

Scene 5

Clarissa (alone)

No. 10. Recitative

Oh, if only you could do it!
If through your tricks, you
could carry hope to the troubled heart,
and silence the pain!
But, oh, I am so afraid.
The joy of life blooms for me no more!

Aria

Sweet delightful, dreams of hope,
how you flood my heart!
You are painting the clouds rosy pink,
you give rest to my pain,
blissfully I want to dream on,
revelling in sweet joy,
which blooms for me in your effervescence—
yet the heart wants to burst my breast.
Ah, how painful
is its beating,
onto my cheeks
run drops of
hot tears!
Ah, all my yearning
knows but one object!

I never understood,
never felt,
such delight,

Solche Schmerzen, Tief im Herzen, Ein solch' Beglücken, Solch' Bedrücken, Als ich in der Liebe fand. [Ich in der Liebe nur empfand.] Nein, nie empfand Ich solch' Entzücken Nie verstand Ich solch' Beglücken, Als durch ihn ich jetzt empfand! Ob es lächle, Ob es grolle, Sei es finster, Sei es licht— Doch was auch das Schicksal wolle, Eines weiß ich Festzuhalten: Wie sich Alles Mög gestalten, Den Geliebten Laß ich nicht!	such pain, deep in the heart, such a delight, such affliction, as I found in love. [I only felt in love.] No, I never felt such delight, I never understood such afflication as I now feel through him! Whether it smiles, whether it growls, be it dark, be it light— yet whatever fate wills, one thing I hold fast: No matter how everything might turn out, I will not leave my beloved!

Scene 6

Vorigen. Laura. Gleich darauf Gomez.

(DIALOG)

LAURA
(*steckt den Kopf durch die Tür*) Herrin, Herrin, hier ist jemand, der Sie sprechen muß!

CLARISSA
Um's Himmelswillen, doch nicht—?

GOMEZ
(*eintretend*) Ich selbst, teure Clarissa!

CLARISSA
Gomez! Gomez! Was wagt Ihr?—Eure Verborgen—nicht zu verlassen—dieses Haus zu betreten!

GOMEZ
Jetzt gilt es nicht mehr meine Sicherheit—es gilt Dein, mein Lebensglück!

CLARISSA
Oh Du mein Geliebter! (*wirft sich an seine Brust*)

LAURA
Herrin!—(*Clarissa beachtet sie nicht.*) Herrin!—(*wie vorher*) Nun—dann werde ich wohl Wache halten müssen, da sie taub und blind zu sein scheinen! (*ab*)

GOMEZ
Wie lange ist's, seit ich Dich nicht Aug' in Auge sah, Geliebte!

Scene 6

As before. Laura. Same with Gomez.

(DIALOGUE)

LAURA
(*sticks her head through the door*) Mistress, mistress, here is someone who must speak with you!

CLARISSA
For heaven's sake, not really—?

GOMEZ
(*entering*) I myself, dear Clarissa!

CLARISSA
Gomez! Gomez! What do you dare?—Your hiding—not to leave—to enter this house!

GOMEZ
Now my safety means nothing more to me—you matter more, my life's happiness!

CLARISSA
Oh, you, my beloved! (*throws herself on his chest*)

LAURA
Mistress!—(*Clarissa doesn't notice her.*) Mistress!—(*as before*) Now, I must then keep watch, since they appear to be deaf and blind! (*leaves*)

GOMEZ
How much time has passed, since I saw you face-to-face, beloved!

CLARISSA
Oh, Gomez, eine Ewigkeit! Und hast Du vernommen, was heut' geschehen? Was heute sich zwischen uns stellt?

GOMEZ
Laura hat mir alles berichtet—aber es soll anders kommen und sollt' ich diesen Don Pinto mit dem Degen aus dem Hause jagen! Du bist mein und sollst keinem Andern angehören so lange ich lebe!

CLARISSA
Ja, Gomez, ewig bin ich Dein und baue fest auf Dich und uns're Liebe!

No. 11. Duett

GOMEZ
Ja, das Wort ich will es sprechen,
Das das Ungemach bezwingt:
Meine Lieb' hält ihr Versprechen,
Was sie hoffend wagt, gelingt!

CLARISSA
Ach, ich seh' mit trübem Blicke
In die Zukunft kummervoll,
Sage, wie dem Mißgeschicke
Uns're Liebe wehren soll?

GOMEZ
Riesenkräfte schafft die Liebe,
Wenn Ihr Gegenliebe lacht;
In das irdische Getriebe
Greift sie ein mit Himmelsmacht.

CLARISSA
Darf ich bauen auf die Liebe?
Diesen Stern, der tröstend wacht—
Der, ob Alles dunkel bliebe,
Doch den Himmel heiter macht!

GOMEZ
Ja, vertrau' ihm!

CLARISSA
Glänzt er immer?

GOMEZ
Niemals schwindet uns sein Schimmer,
Laß uns folgen seinem Licht,
Sei das Dunkel noch so dicht!

CLARISSA
Doch Gefahren—

GOMEZ
Laß sie drohen
Traue mir nur!

CLARISSA
Deinem Herzen!

CLARISSA
Oh, Gomez, an eternity! And have you heard what happened today? What today stands between us?

GOMEZ
Laura reported all of it to me—but it will turn out otherwise, even if I have to chase Don Pinto out of the house with a sword! You are mine and shall not belong to another man as long as I live!

CLARISSA
Yes, Gomez, I am yours forever, and rely on you and our love!

No. 11. Duet

GOMEZ
Yes, I will say the word
that will defeat this trouble:
My love holds its promise,
what it dares by hope will succeed!

CLARISSA
Ah, I see with troubled glances
into the care-filled future!
Tell me how our love should
withstand this misfortune?

GOMEZ
Love makes strength gigantic,
when love requited smiles;
in earthly concerns love
intervenes with heaven's strength.

CLARISSA
Dare I rely on love?
This star that watches consolingly—
even if everything remains dark,
love still makes heaven joyful!

GOMEZ
Yes, I trust it!

CLARISSA
Does this star always shine?

GOMEZ
Never does its splendor set.
Let us follow its light,
even if the darkness is very deep!

CLARISSA
Yet dangers—

GOMEZ
Let them threaten,
only trust me!

CLARISSA
To your heart!

GOMEZ
Hege Hoffnung!

CLARISSA
Unter Schmerzen!
So wie Blumen—

GOMEZ
So wie Blüten—

BEIDE
Sprießen trotz der Stürme Wüthen,
Wächst aus dieser Stunden Grau'n
Lieben, Hoffen und Vertrau'n!

Scene 7

Vorige. Laura (durch die Mitte).

No. 12. Terzett-Finale

LAURA
Geschwind nur von hinnen,
Der Vater naht!

CLARISSA
O, was nun beginnen?

LAURA
Nur Zeit gewinnen
Zu gutem Rath.

GOMEZ
Du, Laura, wirst helfen,
Wir kämpfen zu Dritt.

LAURA
Ist man unter Wölfen,
So heulet man mit.
D'rum listig, verschlagen!

CLARISSA
Wie soll ich's nur ertragen?

GOMEZ
Sei stark und vertraue!

LAURA
Zwar schielt jetzt der Himmel in's Graue,
Doch steiget die Sonne und scheuchet
Die Nebel bald fort.

GOMEZ
Vertrau' meinem Wort!

CLARISSA
Mein Herr und mein Hort!

LAURA
(zu Clarissa)
Doch nun auch fort!

GOMEZ
Keep hope!

CLARISSA
Under pains!
Like the flowers—

GOMEZ
Like the blossoms—

BOTH
But despite raging storms,
thus in these gray hours
grow love, hope, and trust!

Scene 7

As before. Laura (in the middle).

12. Terzett-Finale

LAURA
Leave here quickly,
father is coming!

CLARISSA
Oh, what shall we do now?

LAURA
Only win time
for good counsel.

GOMEZ
You, Laura, will help,
we fight, we three.

LAURA
When you are with wolves,
you howl with them.
Thus, be crafty and cunning!

CLARISSA
How should I endure?

GOMEZ
Be strong and have confidence!

LAURA
Now heaven may appear gray,
yet the sun rises and soon scares
the mists away.

GOMEZ
Trust my word!

CLARISSA
My lord and my treasure!

LAURA
(to Clarissa)
But now go!

GOMEZ
Von Dir mich zu trennen
Zerreißt mir das Leben!

CLARISSA
O könnt ich Dir's nennen
Dies ängstliche Beben!

LAURA
Es wird sich schon geben
Dies Trennen, dies Brennen!
(*zu Clarissa*)
Nur jetzo schon fort!

GOMEZ
Leb' wohl denn, du Theure,
Den Schwur ich erneu're—
Du trau' meinem Wort!

CLARISSA
Leb' wohl, Du mein Lieber,
Wie bliebe ich lieber
Bei Dir hier am Ort.

LAURA
Minuten vergehen,
Hier länger zu stehen
Ist gegen das Wort!
(*alle drei ab*)

(*Ende des zweiten Aufzuges*)

Dritter Aufzug

(*Großer Festsaal in Don Pantaleone's Palast.*)

Scene 1

Laura und die Dienerinnen des Hauses sind beschäftigt den Saal mit Blumen und Guirlanden zu schmücken.

No. 13. Lied mit Chor
LAURA
Schmücket die Halle mit Blüthen und Zweigen,
Rosen und Myrthen in sinnigen Reih'n!

CHOR
Schmücket die Halle mit Blüthen und Zweigen,
Rosen und Myrthen in sinnigen Reih'n!

LAURA UND CHOR
Laßt aus dem Lorbeer Granaten sich neigen,
Flechtet auch wehende Palmen darein.

LAURA
Wonnig begrüßen von Bogen und Wänden
Schwebende Ranken das bräutliche Paar.

GOMEZ
To be separated from you
tears my life apart!

CLARISSA
O, if I could only name for you
this frightful trembling!

LAURA
It will soon pass,
this separation, this burning!
(*to Clarissa*)
Just go!

GOMEZ
Farewell, then, my treasure,
I renew my oath—
and you, trust my word!

CLARISSA
Farewell, my love.
I would so much rather
stay with you here.

LAURA
Minutes pass,
to stay here longer
goes against our agreement!
(*all three leave*)

(*end of the second act*)

Act Three

(*Great Festival Hall in Don Pantaleone's place.*)

Scene 1

Laura and the women servants of the house are occupied in decorating the hall with flowers and garlands.

No. 13. Song with Chorus
LAURA
Decorate the halls with blossoms and branches,
roses and myrtle in decorative rows!

CHORUS
Decorate the halls with blossoms and branches,
roses and myrtle in decorative rows!

LAURA AND CHORUS
Let pomegrantes bend from the laurels,
and weave gracious palms among them.

LAURA
Runners suspended from arches and walls,
sweetly greet the bridal couple.

LAURA UND CHOR
Duftende Blumen mit liebenden Händen
Streut auf Pfad ihm zum Hochzeitsaltar,
Schmücket die Halle, die blühenden Spenden
Bringen wir freudig den Glücklichen dar!
(*Sie sind fertig geworden und betrachten nun ihr Werk.*)
Nun seht, es ist gelungen!
Wie lustig, herrlich, prächtig!
Ei seht, wie wunderschön!

Scene 2

Die Vorigen. Haushofmeister (durch die Mitte).

Dialog
HAUSHOFMEISTER
Fort, hinaus, Ihr Mädchen, Don Pinto de Fonseca kommt hierher!

DIE MÄDCHEN
Was—Don Pinto? Den wollen wir sehen! Den müssen wir sehen!

HAUSHOFMEISTER
Hinaus, habe ich gesagt, sonst soll gleich ein heiliges Mohrenkreuzschockdonnerwetter—

(*Die Mädchen laufen in komischem Schrecken nach allen Seiten davon. Laura hat sich inter ein Pflazenbouquet versteckt, wo der Haushofmeister sie nicht bemerkt. Dieser nach rechts ab. Laura macht spottende Gesten hinter ihm drein.*)

LAURA
Ich werde diesen Don Pinto doch sehen, auch ohne Ihr gütige Erlaubnis, Herr Grimmbart!

Scene 3

Die Vorigen. Gaston und Ambrosio (durch die Mitte). Sie betrachten die festliche Halle.

No. 14. Duett
GASTON UND AMBROSIO
Nun da sind wir, hier nur eben
Scheint man Mühe sich zu geben
Große Ehr' uns anzuthun!

GASTON
Frohe Anstalt allerwegen,
Doch kam Niemand uns entgegen,
Alles scheint im Schlaf zu ruh'n.

AMBROSIO
Auch der Alte, der vom Thore
Uns so höflich hierher führte
Lag wohl just auf einem Ohre.
Doch in seinem Lächeln spürte
Ich ein freundliches Vergnügen.

LAURA AND CHORUS
Strew fragrant flowers with loving hands
on the aisle to the wedding altar,
decorate the halls; we joyfully bring
blossoming presents to the happy ones.
(*They are finished and now regard their work.*)
Now see, we succeeded!
How merry, noble, splendid!
Oh, see how wonderful!

Scene 2

As before. Steward (through the middle).

Dialogue
STEWARD
Away, out, girls, Don Pinto de Fonseca arrives!

MAIDENS
What—Don Pinto? We want to see him! Him we must see!

STEWARD
Out, I said, or rather, should like holy Moor-cross-shocking-thunderstorm—

(*The maidens run out on all sides with comic cries of fright. Laura has hidden herself behind a bouquet where the steward cannot see her. He exits right. Laura makes mocking gestures at him as he leaves.*)

LAURA
I will yet see this Don Pinto, even without your permission, Herr Grimmbart!

Scene 3

As before. Gaston and Ambrosio (through the middle). They regard the festive hall.

No. 14. Duet
GASTON AND AMBROSIO
Now that we are here, it only
appears that someone took the
trouble to do us a great honor!

GASTON
Joyful preparations on all counts,
yet no one comes to meet us,
everyone appears to be asleep.

AMBROSIO
Also, the old man who conducted us
here from the gate
must have just taken a nap.
Yet in his smile I detected
a friendly demeanor.

BEIDE
Ei, es wird sich alles fügen.
Harren wir getrost der Dinge,
Die sich bergen hier im Hause,
Harren, daß das Werk gelinge.

AMBROSIO
Kommt es nur zum Hochzeitsschmause,
Da will ich recht lustig springen!
Kastagnetten hör' ich klingen,
[Dum trr um trr um trr um tum,]
Flöt' und Clarinetten singen
Dideldui, Dideldui!

GASTON
Doch als dann—

AMBROSIO
Wenn—

GASTON
Ja! Wenn!

BEIDE
Ei, was hilft das Überlegen
Frischen Muthes vorwärts nun;
Jeder Schwank kommt ja gelegen
Uns'rer fröhlichen Natur.
Nur ein Thor der Zukunft harrt,
Weisen lacht die Gegenwart!

Dialog
AMBROSIO
Herr, sind wir dann nicht rechte, echte Thoren?

GASTON
Wieso, mein törichter Ambrosio?

AMBROSIO
Ja, erwarten wir denn nicht alles von der Zukunft?

GASTON
Kerl, Du bist ein Galgen-Philosoph!

AMBROSIO
Um Gotteswillen, Herr, nennt nicht dieses entsetzliche Wort!

GASTON
Nun, nun, nicht so ängstlich, ehrlicher Ambrosio, hier ist ja kein Galgen in Sicht!

AMBROSIO
(*sich umblickend*) Gott sei Dank, nein! Im Gegenteil, recht feierlich und festlich sieht's hier aus! Alle Achtung!—(*Er geht umher, findet hinter dem Bouquet Laura und zieht sie hervor.*) Alle Liebesgötter! Wen haben wir denn hier?

BOTH
Oh, everything will work out.
Let us wait patiently on things
that are concealed in this house.
Wait, so that the work succeeds.

AMBROSIO
When it comes to the wedding feast,
there will I dance merrily!
I hear castanettes ring out,
[Dum trr um trr um trr um tum,]
flute and clarinet sing
Dideldui, Dideldui!

GASTON
Yet then—

AMBROSIO
If—

GASTON
Yes! If!

BOTH
Oh, what use is thinking about it;
let's go on with fresh courage now;
each prank suits
our joyful nature.
Only a fool waits for the future,
the present smiles on the wise.

Dialogue
AMBROSIO
Master, are we then not really truly fools?

GASTON
How so, my foolish Ambrosio?

AMBROSIO
Yeah, do we not expect everything from the future?

GASTON
Knave, you are a gallows-philosopher!

AMBROSIO
As God wills it, master, don't mention that terrible word!

GASTON
Now, now, not so nervously, honest Ambrosio, there is not a single gallows in sight!

AMBROSIO
(*looking around*) Thank God, no! On the other hand, things seem to be quite solemn and festive here! My compliments!—(*He goes around, finds Laura behind the bouquet and pulls her forward.*) All the gods of love! Whom do we have here?

LAURA Ei, Ihr kecker Mensch—hier in unser'm eig'nen Hause?	**LAURA** Oh, you fresh, young man—here in our own house?
GASTON Wer bist Du, schönes Kind?	**GASTON** Who are you, beautiful child?
LAURA Seid Ihr Don Pinto, schöner Herr?	**LAURA** Are you Don Pinto, handsome master?
GASTON Frage gegen Frage, Antwort gegen Antwort! Also Ja! Nun und Du?	**GASTON** Question for question, answer for answer! Well, yes! And you?
LAURA Ich bin Donna Clarissa's und bald auch Eure ergebenste Dienerin!	**LAURA** I am one of Donna Clarissa's maids and soon your most humble servant!
GASTON Donna Clarissa? Hat die Dich hier in Hinterhalt gelegt?	**GASTON** Donna Clarissa? Has she sent you here to spy?
LAURA Nein, Herr, ich suchte hier etwas.—	**LAURA** No, sir, I was looking for something here.—
GASTON Ach so, ja, ich verstehe!—Du hast doch gefunden?	**GASTON** Ah, so, yes, I understand!—Have you yet found it?
LAURA Ja, Herr, darum (*sie macht ihm einen Knix*) Gott befohlen!	**LAURA** Yes, sir, and therefore (*she curtsies to him*) Good-bye!
GASTON Auf Wiedersehen, mein schönes Kind; Deiner Herrin meinen Gruß!	**GASTON** Farewell, my beautiful child; give your mistress my greetings!
LAURA Werd's berichten! (*Sie wendet sich zum Gehen.*)	**LAURA** I will convey them! (*She turns to go.*)
AMBROSIO (*vertritt ihr den Weg*) Ich habe auch gesucht—und—habe auch gefunden! Ich bin Ambrosio!	**AMBROSIO** (*stops her on the way*) I have also sought—and found! I am Ambrosio!
LAURA Sehr erfreut!	**LAURA** Very pleased!
AMBROSIO Doch ich bin ganz entzückt—	**AMBROSIO** Yet I am entirely enchanted—
LAURA Noch mehr erfreut!	**LAURA** Even more pleased!
AMBROSIO Von Eurem Liebreiz—Eure Schönheit, hold Inez!	**AMBROSIO** By your charms—Your beauty, dear Inez!
LAURA Ei seht doch! Inez hieß wohl die Letzte die Ihr liebtet?	**LAURA** Oh see here! Inez is the name of the last one whom you loved?
AMBROSIO Beim Himmel! Ihr sollt die Letzte sein!	**AMBROSIO** By heaven! You should be the last one!

GASTON
Ambrosio, schwöre nicht—Mädchen, trau ihm nicht!

No. 15. Terzettino (Canon)

AMBROSIO
Mädchen ich leide heiße Liebespein,
Dein schelmisches Auge flößt mir sie ein!
Nicht nur süße Schmeicheleien
Will dies weiche Herz Dir weihen.
Glaube, Mädchen, meinen Worten
Niemals wird es mich gereu'n!

GASTON
Mädchen, ach meide
Männerschmeichelei'n,
Die kosenden Worte schläfern Dich ein.
Statt der süßen Schmeicheleien
Hörst Du: "Mama! Papa!" schreien.
Glaube, Mädchen, meinem Worte
Sicher wird es Dich gereu'n!

LAURA
Mädchen erleiden
Männerschmeichelei'n
Wie Rosen die Schwüre bunter Käferlein.
All' die süßen Schmeicheleien
Können kein Vertrauen leihen.
Mädchen lachen solcher Worte,
Wenn sie sich auch d'ran erfreu'n!

AMBROSIO
Mädchen ich leide heiße Liebespein,
Dein schelmisches Auge flößt mir sie ein!
Nicht nur süße Schmeicheleien
Will dies weiche Herz Dir weihen.
Glaube, Mädchen, meinen Worten
Niemals wird es mich gereu'n!

GASTON
Mädchen, ach meide
Männerschmeichelei'n,
Die kosenden Worte schläfern Dich ein.
Statt der süßen Schmeicheleien
Hörst Du: "Mama! Papa!" schreien.
Glaube, Mädchen, meinem Worte
Sicher wird es Dich gereu'n!

LAURA
(*zu Gaston spottend*)
"Mädchen, ach meide
Männerschmeichelei'n,
Die kosenden Worte, Mädchen, schläfern Dich ein!"
(*Sie springt lachend von dannen, ab nach rechts.*)

GASTON
Ambrosio, don't swear—Maiden, don't trust him!

No. 15. Terzettino (Canon)

AMBROSIO
Maiden, I suffer the intense pains of love,
your impish eyes affect me so!
This weak heart wants to dedicate to you
not only sweet flatteries.
Maiden, believe my words,
never will I regret it!

GASTON
Maiden, oh, avoid
men's flatteries,
the caressing words lull you to sleep.
Instead of sweet flatteries
you shall hear someone cry: "Mama! Papa!"
Maiden, believe my word,
you will surely regret it!

LAURA
Maidens suffer
men's flatteries,
as roses suffer the oaths of multi-colored beetles.
All the sweet flatteries
can lend no trust at all.
Maidens laugh at such words
even if they enjoy them!

AMBROSIO
Maiden, I suffer the intense pains of love,
your impish eyes affect me so!
This weak heart wants to dedicate to you
not only sweet flatteries.
Maiden, believe my words,
never will I regret it!

GASTON
Maiden, oh, avoid
men's flatteries,
the caressing words lull you to sleep.
Instead of sweet flatteries
you should hear someone cry: "Mama! Papa!"
Maiden, believe my word,
you will surely regret it!

LAURA
(*to Gaston, mocking*)
"Maiden, oh, avoid
men's flatteries,
the caressing words, maiden, put you to sleep."
(*She jumps away laughing and exits stage right.*)

Scene 4

Die Vorigen ohne Laura

Dialog

GASTON

Hahaha, ein schelmisches Ding! Die ist Dir gewachsen, tapferer Ambrosio!

GASTON

(*spottend*) Ha! Welch ein furchtbarer Zorn!

No. 16. Ariette

(*Während des Vorspiels desselben geht Ambrosio zornig auf und nieder.*)

AMBROSIO

(*parodiert seinen eigenen Zorn. Endlich schägt er ein Schnippchen und singt.*)

[Vers 1]

Ein Mädchen verloren
Was macht man sich d'raus?
Man sucht sich in Spanien
Ein' Andere aus!
Und täuscht uns auch diese,
Was liegt denn daran?
Es kommt heut' zu Tage
Ein Schock auf den Mann!
La, la, la! La, la, la!
(*Er tanzt während des Singens.*)

Vers 2

Man muß in der Liebe
Nicht einseitig sein!
Man hält es am besten
Mit Zweien und Drei'n.
Denn kränkt uns die Eine,
Wie leicht hat man's dann!
Man wartet ganz ruhig
Bis sie kommt daran!
La, la la! La, la la!

Vers 3

Ich rath' Euch, Ihr Männer,
Schwört nie einen Eid!
Ich rath Euch, als Kenner,
Sonst fängt Euch die Maid!
Denn wird sie Euch lästig,
So sitzet Ihr d'ran.
Es läßt Euch kein Mädchen
Leicht los einen Mann!
La, la, la! La, la, la!

Scene 4

As before, without Laura

Dialogue

GASTON

Hahaha, an implish thing! She is a match for you, brave Ambrosio!

GASTON

(*mocking*) Ha! What fearsome anger!

No. 16. Arietta

(*During the introduction, Ambrosio walks up and down angrily.*)

AMBROSIO

(*parodies his own anger. Finally he snaps his fingers and sings.*)

[Verse 1]

A maiden lost,
what do you care?
In Spain you look for
another one!
And if this one also deceived us,
what does it matter?
These days there are
sixty for each man!
La, la, la! La, la, la!
(*He dances while singing.*)

Verse 2

In love you must not be
one-sided!
It is best if one deals by
twos or threes.
If one offends us,
you then have it easy!
You wait quietly
until another comes along!
La, la, la! La, la, la!

Verse 3

I advise you, men,
never swear an oath!
I advise you as one who knows,
or the maiden will catch you!
If she becomes a burden to you,
then you are caught.
No maiden easily
lets a man go!
La, la, la! La, la, la!

Scene 5

Die Vorigen. Laura führt Gomez herein.

DIALOG

LAURA
Da sind sie!

GOMEZ
Ich werde ihm hier entgegentreten! Du harre hier und berichte dann Deiner Herrin!

LAURA
(*hält sich während des Folgenden in der Nähe der Sprechenden, sodaß sie alles hören kann*)

GOMEZ
(*tritt mit einer höflichen Verbeugung an Gaston heran*) Don Pinto de Fonseca?

GASTON
(*erst befremdend, dann sich besinnend*) Ja, der bin ich!

GOMEZ
Ich heiße Don Gomez Freiros—meine Familie gehört dem ältesten Adel von Madrid an. Ich trete Euch gegenüber, edler Don Pinto, wie ein Edelmann dem andern: mit vollster Offenheit und dem unbedingtesten Vertrauen auf Eure ritterliche Gesinnung.

GASTON
Verlaßt Euch auf sie, Don Gomez und glaubt, daß ich Eurer Offenheit ebenso aufrichtig begegnen werde.

GOMEZ
Don Pinto, Ihr kommt hierher in Don Pantaleone's Haus mit mächtigen Mitteln ausgerüstet, um ein Glück zu gewinnen, das Ihr noch nicht ermessen könnt, da Ihr Donna Clarissa noch nicht gesehen!

GASTON
Was soll Donna Clarissa hier?

GOMEZ
Ich liebe Clarissa und werde wieder geliebt!

GASTON
Fürwahr, Don Gomez, Ihr seid sehr kühn und auf Eure Beleidigung kann ich nur mit meinem Degen erwidern.

GOMEZ
Ich will Euch nicht beleidigen, Don Pinto, und tat ich's doch durch mein Geständnis, so biete ich Euch jede Genugtuung.

GASTON
Aber was verlangt Ihr?

Scene 5

As before. Laura leads Gomez in.

DIALOGUE

LAURA
There they are!

GOMEZ
I will meet him here. You wait here and then report to your mistress!

LAURA
(*in the following stays nearby, so that she can hear everything*)

GOMEZ
(*approaches Gaston with a polite bow*) Don Pinto de Fonseca?

GASTON
(*first unknowing, then aware*) Yes, I am he!

GOMEZ
I am called Don Gomez Freiros—my family belongs to the oldest aristocracy in Madrid. I am meeting you, noble Pinto, as one gentleman to another: with full openness and absolute trust in your knightly sensibility.

GASTON
You can rely on it, Don Gomez, and believe that I will meet your openness sincerely.

GOMEZ
Don Pinto, you come to Don Pantaleone's house with powerful resources to win happiness that you cannot even measure, since you have not yet seen Donna Clarissa!

GASTON
What does Donna Clarissa have to do with it?

GOMEZ
I love Clarissa and she loves me in return!

GASTON
Truly, Don Gomez, you are courageous, and I can reply to your insult only with my sword.

GOMEZ
I do not want to insult you, Don Pinto, and if I did so through my admission, then I offer to you every satisfaction.

GASTON
What do you demand?

No. 17. Rondo-Terzett

GOMEZ
Ihr, der so edel, als wahrer Ritter
Treu' bewahret Ehr' und hohen Sinn,
Ihr wolltet trennen zwei treue Herzen,
Reinstes Liebesglück opfern dahin?
Vermöcht' mein heißes Fleh'n Euch zu bewegen,
Ihr trüg't in Euch den schönsten Lohn!
O gebt Gehör den bessern Trieben
Gönnt mir, was sich zu mir gewandt,
Das höchste Gut, das mir geblieben:
Clarissen's Liebe, ihre Hand!

GASTON
Was fällt Euch ein, mein Herr Rittersmann?
Ich sollte Euch weichen auf freier Bahn?
Gebt acht, daß Ihr Euch nur nicht Übel versteht,
Man könnte euch zeigen, wie man den Spaß versteht?
Ich halte Clarissen, ich halte sie fest!

AMBROSIO
(*bei Seite*)
Hört doch an,
Wie er prahlen kann!
Ja, halt sie mir fest,
Daß sie Dich nicht losläßt!

GOMEZ
Ward je ein zartes, holdes Regen
Seligster Lieb' Euch bewußt,
Hat je in heißen, mächt'gen Schlägen
Das Herz Euch geklopfet in der Brust,
So müßt Ihr meines Innern Drang verst'hen,
Erkennen meine höchste Noth!
Bei jeder Hoffnung Eures Lebens,
Bei Eurer Ahnen Wappenschild,
Beim Siege Eures kühnsten Strebens
Beschwör' ich Euch: bezeigt Euch mild!

GASTON
Nun denn, wohlan!
Mein Herr Rittersmann,
Ich trete zurück,
Euch begünstigt das Glück!
Ich wünsche zu Hochzeit
Euch viel Vergnügen!
Clarissa wird selig
Am Herzen Euch liegen,
Wird jauchzend vor Glück!
[Sich an Euren Busen schmiegen!]

ALLE DREI
[GASTON]
Nun denn wohlan!
Mein Herr Rittersmann,
Ich trete zurück,
Euch begünstigt das Glück!
Ich wünsche zur Hochzeit
Euch viel Vergnügen!

No. 17. Rondo-Terzett

GOMEZ
You, who nobly as a true knight,
faithfully preserve honor and high nobility,
you would separate two true hearts,
and thereby sacrifice purest happiness in love?
If my fervent imploring could move you,
you would carry within you the most wonderful reward!
Oh, listen to your better instincts,
allow me, what belongs to me,
the highest good, that remains with me:
Clarissa's love, her hand!

GASTON
What do you think, my noble knight?
That I should yield to you when I have a clear road?
Watch out that you don't bring evil upon yourself;
people might show you how they take such jokes!
I hold Clarissa, I hold her firm!

AMBROSIO
(*aside*)
Listen to him,
how he can boast!
Hold her firmly for me—
so that she does not let go of you!

GOMEZ
If you ever knew the tender, loving movement
of most blissful love,
if your heart ever beat in passionate,
powerful strokes in your breast,
then you must understand my inner feelings,
and recognize my highest suffering!
by all the hope of your life,
by your ancestral coat of arms,
by the victory of your most valiant striving,
I implore you: show yourself to be merciful!

GASTON
Now then, well,
my good knight,
I step back,
fortune smiles on you!
I wish you much joy
for the wedding!
Clarissa will joyfully
embrace you and
will sing with happiness!
[and press herself to your chest!]

ALL THREE
[GASTON]
Now then, well,
my good knight,
I step back,
fortune smiles on you!
I wish you much joy
for the wedding!

Clarissa wird selig Am Herzen Euch liegen, Wird jauchzend vor Glück, Sich an Euren Busen schmiegen! Dann haltet Clarissa, Dann haltet sie fest!	Clarissa will be joyful as you lie on her heart, and will revel in happiness and press herself to your chest! Then hold Clarissa, then hold her firm!

GOMEZ / GOMEZ

Er tritt zurück! Überschwenglich Glück! Welch'e Glück er tritt zurück! Clarissa ist mein! Clarissa wird selig Am Herzen mir liegen, Ja selig an mich sich schmiegen! Ich halte Clarissen, Ich halte sie fest!	He stepped back! Abundant fortune! What luck that he stepped back! Clarissa is mine! Clarissa will happily embrace me, yes, happily caress me! I hold Clarissa, I hold her fast!

AMBROSIO / AMBROSIO

(*bei Seite*) / (*aside*)

Meinetwegen Glück und Segen! Glücklicher Mann, Der sie gewann Halt sie nur fest, Daß sie Dich nicht losläßt! Ob Gaston, ob Gomez, Was kann daran liegen, Von Beiden sie kriegen. Dies Eine steht fest, Dies Eine steht fest!	All right! Happiness and blessings! Fortunate man, who won her, only hold her fast, so that she does not let go of you! Whether Gaston, whether Gomez, what can it matter, since she catches both. This thing I know, this thing is true!

Dialog / Dialogue

GASTON

Doch nun sagt mir, Don Gomez, seid Ihr sicher, daß Clarissens Vater grade Euch als Eidam annimmt, wenn ich zurücktrete?	Yet now tell me, Don Gomez, are you certain that Clarissa's father will take you as a son-in-law if I step back?

GOMEZ

Ihr habt sehr recht, das ist die zweite grosse Schwierigkeit! Er kennt mich nicht, er hat mich nie gesehen—und Clarissa schildert ihn als einen Eisenkopf!	You are right, that is the second great difficulty! He doesn't know me, he has never even seen me—and Clarissa describes him as having a head of iron!

GASTON

Er kennt Euch nicht und hat Euch nie gesehen?	He doesn't know you and has never even seen you?

GOMEZ

Niemals!	Never!

GASTON

So kann ich Euch denn weiter helfen! Seid Ihr bereit, den alten Herrn zu überlisten?	Well, then I can help you along! Are you prepared to outwit the old gentleman?

GOMEZ

Ich scheue keine Mittel, Clarissa zu gewinnen—wenn es kein schlechtes ist!	I spare no means to win Clarissa—unless it is dishonorable!

GASTON

Hört selbst. Hier ist der Brief meines Vaters, der mich bei Don Pantaleone einführt—hier nehmt ihn.—Ihr seid Don Pinto de Fonseca!	Listen! Here is the letter of my father, which introduces me to Don Pantaleone—here take it.—You be Don Pinto de Fonseca!

GOMEZ
Wie—ich Don Pinto?

GASTON
Ja, Ihr seid Don Pinto und werdet so Clarissens Gatte!—Ist sie erst Euer Weib, so kann Euch keine Macht der Welt mehr trennen. Dann nennt Ihr Euren wahren Namen und Don Pantaleone muss sich wohl oder übel fügen!—Doch rat ich Eile!

GOMEZ
(*ihn umarmend*) O mein Retter, mein Beglücker! Noch heute soll Clarissa mir angehören.

GASTON
So lebt denn wohl, Don Gomez, möge Euch das Glück zur Seite steh'n.

GOMEZ
Wie, Ihr wolltet mich verlassen? Bedarf ich nicht Eurer Hilfe und Eures Rates auf Schritt und Tritt? Wie, wenn Don Pantaleone nach Verhältnissen Eurer Familie fragt und ich wüsste keinen Bescheid?

GASTON
(*für sich*) O weh, was weiss ich denn von den Fonsecas! Nun heisst es erfinderisch sein! (*laut*) Nun wohl, so bleibe ich an Eurer Seite, als einer Eurer Freunde. Nennt mich Don Gaston Viratos, wenn Ihr wollt.

GOMEZ
O, Dank, tausend Dank!

GASTON
Nun schnell, zieht Donna Clarissa in's Geheimnis!

GOMEZ
So geh' denn, Laura, und melde Deiner Herrin—(*spricht leise mit ihr weiter*)

AMBROSIO
(*zu Gaston*) Nun Herr, mit Donna Clarissa war es also nichts? Wie gewonnen, so zerronnen!

GASTON
Es ist sehr gut so, Ambrosio! Hatte ich doch schon Gewissensbisse ob des gar zu tollen Streiches! Und unsern Spass haben wir ja doch dabei, wenn der kalbsgesichtige Don Pinto um die holde Clarissa geprellt wird!

AMBROSIO
Jawohl, bravo, bravo! Und wir trösten uns schon! (*Laura ab*)

GOMEZ
(*zu Gaston zurückkehrend*) Edler Don Pinto—

GASTON
Don Gaston, wenn ich bitten darf—

GOMEZ
How—I, Don Pinto?

GASTON
Yes, you be Don Pinto and thus become Clarissa's beloved!—once she is your wife, no power in the world can separate you. Then you take your true name and Don Pantaleone must sooner or later give in. But I advise speed!

GOMEZ
(*hugs him*) Oh, my savior, my bringer of good luck! Yet today Clarissa will belong to me.

GASTON
So farewell, then, Don Gomez, and may fortune be at your side.

GOMEZ
What will you leave me? Don't I need your help and your advice for every step I take? What if Don Pantaleone asks about conditions in your family and I would have no reply?

GASTON
(*to himself*) Alas, what do I know then about the Fonsecas! Now I must be inventive! (*aloud*) Well now, I will remain at your side as one of your friends. Call me Don Gaston Viratos if you will.

GOMEZ
Oh, thank you, a thousand thanks!

GASTON
Now quick, let Donna Clarrisa in on the secret!

GOMEZ
So go then, Laura, and tell your mistress—(*speaks softly to her further*)

AMBROSIO
(*to Gaston*) Now sir, nothing came of Donna Clarrisa? Easy come, easy go!

GASTON
That's all right, Ambrosio! I already had compunctions because it was too crazy a prank! And we will have fun anyway, if the calf-faced Don Pinto gets cheated of the lovely Clarissa!

AMBROSIO
Oh yes, bravo, bravo! And we shall console ourselves! (*Laura leaves*)

GOMEZ
(*going back to Gaston*) Noble Don Pinto—

GASTON
Don Gaston, if I may ask—

GOMEZ Edler Don Gaston, ich hoffe freudig, es wird gelingen!	GOMEZ Noble Don Gaston, I joyfully hope that it will succeed!

Scene 6 / Scene 6

Die Vorigen. Die Dienerschaft tritt ein. / *As before. The servants step in.*

No. 18. Chor / No. 18. Chorus

CHOR
Habt Ihr es denn schon vernommen?
Eben ist er angekommen!
Welcher ist es?—Jener da!
Nein, der And're! Freilich! Ja!
Still doch, still, da naht sie schon!
Welch ein schöner junger Ritter,
Welche Haltung, welcher Blick!
Was wird wohl Clarissa sagen
Wenn sie den Verlobten schaut?
Einen solchen Mann gewinnen
Ist ein selt'nes, grosses Glück!
Kann ein Mädchen sich besinnen
Ihn zu nehmen vom Geschick?
(*Die Tür öffnet sich wieder.*)
Still doch, da naht sie schon!

CHORUS
Have you already heard?
He has just arrived!
Which is it?—This one!
No, the other! Of course! Yes!
Yet quiet, quiet, she already draws near!
What a handsome young knight,
such bearing, such gaze!
What will Clarissa say
when she sees her betrothed?
To win such a man
is rare, great luck!
Can a maiden have second thoughts,
if fate gives her such a man?
(*The door opens further.*)
Yet quiet, she already draws near!

AMBROSIO
(*gesprochen*) Ei, seht, da kommt der längst erwartete Empfang!

AMBROSIO
(*spoken*) Oh, the long-awaited welcome!

GASTON
(*desgleichen*) Still, Bursch, jetzt wird es Ernst!

GASTON
(*the same*) Quiet, knave, now it's getting serious!

CHOR
Segen diesem schönen Bunde,
Segen über diese Stunde!
Glück, Segen und Heil auf dieses Haus!
Seht sie naht! Heil und höchstes Glück!
Heil Clarissa, Pantaleone
Heil dem edlen Schwiegersohne
Den Euch diese Stunde schenkt!
Seid gegrüsst, willkommen, Heil!

CHORUS
Blessings on this beautiful union,
blessings on this hour!
Fortune, blessings, and hail to this house!
See, she draws near! Hail and best of luck!
Hail Clarissa, Pantaleone
hail to the noble son-in-law
whom this hour gives you!
Be greeted, welcome, hail!

(*Don Pantaleone hat die festlich geschmückte Clarissa feierlich hereingeführt und bleibt bis zum Schluss der Musik inmitten der Dienerschaft würdevoll stehen.*)

(*Don Pantaleone has solemnly led in the festively clad Clarissa, and remains standing to the end of the music, surrounded by his servants.*)

Dialog / Dialogue

PANTALEONE
(*auf Gomez zugehend*) Seid mir willkomm Don Pinto! An Eurer edlen Haltung sehe ich, dass Ihr ein Fonseca seid.

PANTALEONE
(*going to Gomez*) Welcome Don Pinto! From your noble bearing I see that you are a Fonseca.

GOMEZ
Ich grüsse Euch, edler Herr, voll Ehrfurcht! Hier der Brief meines Vaters, der mich in Euer Vertrauen und in Euer Haus einführt.

GOMEZ
I greet you, noble sir, with full respect. Here is the letter of my father, which introduces me to your trust and your house.

PANTALEONE
(*der Brief betrachtend*) Sie sind's, die wohlbekannten Schriftzüge—und hier das stolze Wappen der Fonsecas.

PANTALEONE
(*examining the letter*) This is the familiar handwriting— and here the proud coat-of-arms of the Fonsecas. Hail

Heil Euch, Don Pinto, dass Ihr es in Ehren führen dürft—Heil Dir, mein Kind, dass Du unter seinem Ruhm—und ehrenreichen Zeichen leben sollst! (*Er erbricht den Brief und liest.*) Alles so, wie mir Euer edler Vater es im Voraus schon gemeldet. Aus jedem seiner Worte erkenn' ich ihn wieder. Seht, Don Pinto, wie es mich freut, an dem Sohne das vergelten zu können, was mir der Vater getan. (*Er führt Clarissa Gomez feierlich zu.*) So nehmt sie denn hin mit meinem Segen! Und Du, mein Kind, sei glücklich in den Armen dieses edlen Mannes.

CLARISSA
O, Vater, unendlich glücklich!

(*Laura und Blumenmädchen aus dem Chor treten mit Blumenkörben und einem Myrtenkranz hervor, um dem Paare zu huldigen.*)

No. 19. Terzett
CHOR
Mit lieblichen Blumen,
Mit duftenden Blüthen
Begrüßt Euch der Mädchen frohlockende Schaar.
Sie winden der Holden
Die bräutlichen Zweige
Frisch grünender Myrthe in's lockige Haar!
(*Kaum haben sie geendigt als durch den Haupteingang der Haushofmeister hereinstürzt.*)

Dialog
HAUSHOFMEISTER
(*zu Pantaleone*) Herr, Herr, draußen ist Einer, der sich auch Don Pinto nennt!

PANTALEONE
Schafskopf!

HAUSHOFMEISTER
Das habe ich ihm auch schon gesagt. Er läßt sich aber nicht zurückhalten; hier ist er schon!

Scene 7

Die Vorigen. Don Pinto schreitet gewichtig und aufgeblasen durch den Haupteingang herein. Don Pantaleone tritt würdevoll entgegen.

No. 20. Ensemble—Finale A
PANTALEONE
Was wollt Ihr?
Wer seid Ihr?
Was sucht Ihr?

CHOR
Was wollt Ihr?
Wer seid Ihr?
Was sucht Ihr?

---

to you, Don Pinto, that you may bring honor to it—hail to you, my child, that you will live under its fame and noble emblem! (*He opens the letter and reads.*) Everything is just as your noble father told me in advance. From each of his words I recognize him. See, Don Pinto, how it pleases me, to be able to pay back to the son what the father has done for me. (*He leads Clarissa solemnly to Gomez.*) So take her, then, with my blessing! And you, my child, be happy in the arms of this noble man.

CLARISSA
Oh, father, endless joy!

(*Laura and the flower-girls step out of the chorus with baskets of flowers and a myrtle wreath to pay homage to the couple.*)

No. 19. Terzett
CHORUS
With lovely flowers,
with fragrant blossoms
the joyful group of maidens greet you.
They weave bridal vines into the
hair of the beatiful one,
fresh green myrtle in her locks!
(*Hardly have they ended, when the steward enters through the main doorway.*)

Dialogue
STEWARD
(*to Pantaleone*) Sir, sir, there is someone outside who is also named Don Pinto!

PANTALEONE
Fool!

STEWARD
I told him that already. But he doesn't want to go away; here he is already!

Scene 7

As before. Don Pinto steps self-importantly and arrogantly through the main entrance. Don Pantaleone approaches him in a dignified manner.

No. 20. Ensemble—Finale A
PANTALEONE
What do you want?
Who are you?
What are you seeking?

CHORUS
What do you want?
Who are you?
What are you seeking?

GASTON (*bei Seite*) Nun, ich wasche meine Händ', Jetzo hat der Spaß ein End'!	**GASTON** (*aside*) I wash my hands of it, now the joke has an end!
PINTO Ich bin Don Pinto— Don Pinto de Fonseca!	**PINTO** I am Don Pinto— Don Pinto de Fonseca!
CLARISSA, LAURA, GOMEZ, UND PANTALEONE Wie? Don Pinto de Fonseca?	**CLARISSA, LAURA, GOMEZ, AND PANTALEONE** How? Don Pinto de Fonseca?
CHOR Wie? Don Pinto de Fonseca?	**CHORUS** How? Don Pinto de Fonseca?
PINTO Und ich suche meine Braut!	**PINTO** And I seek my bride!
CLARISSA UND LAURA Was will dieser dicke Mann? Ist das erhört—er wär' Don Pinto?	**CLARISSA AND LAURA** What does this fat man want? Have you ever heard such a thing—he would be Don Pinto?
GOMEZ Dies wär' Pinto, Pinto de Fonseca?	**GOMEZ** This would be Pinto, Pinto de Fonseca?
CHOR Er wär' Pinto—er ist toll! Fort, hinaus!	**CHORUS** He would be Pinto—that's crazy! Away, get out!
PINTO (*eingeschüchtert, doch noch sehr aufgeblasen*) Ich bin Pinto de Fonseca Und ich suche meine Braut! Ja, ich bin Pinto de Fonseca Und Clarissen's Anverlobter!	**PINTO** (*a bit scared, but still very arrogant*) I am Pinto de Fonseca and I seek my bride! Yes, I am Pinto de Fonseca and Clarissa's betrothed!
CLARISSA Dieser wär' mein Bräutigam?	**CLARISSA** This one would be my bridegroom?
LAURA Dies Clarissens Bräutigam?	**LAURA** This is Clarissa's bridegroom?
GOMEZ Na! ein schöner Bräutigam!	**GOMEZ** Well! A handsome bridegroom!
PANTALEONE Dieser Schurke! Dieser Schurke!	**PANTALEONE** This rascal! This scoundrel!
CHOR Dies Clarissen's Anverlobter? Dies Clarissens Bräutigam? Dies Don Pinto?	**CHORUS** This is Clarissa's Betrothed? This is Clarissa's bridegroom? This is Don Pinto?
PINTO (*zu Clarissa*) Sapperlot, Sapperlot! Ihr seid zum Verstand verlieren, Vor Entzücken bin ich todt!	**PINTO** (*to Clarissa*) The dickens, the dickens! You are so beautiful that one might lose one's reason, I am thrilled to death!

GASTON (*bei Seite zu Ambrosio*) Schau' doch hin, was er gelernt!	**GASTON** (*aside to Ambrosio*) See what he has learned!
AMBROSIO (*bei Seite und wie im ersten Akt parodierend*) Welche Kühnheit!	**AMBROSIO** (*aside and parodying as in the first act*) Such courage!
GASTON (*bei Seite zu Ambrosio*) Ganz genau wie wir's probirt!	**GASTON** (*aside to Ambrosio*) Just as we rehearsed!
PINTO (*mit vor Aufregung umschlagender Stimme, vor Clarissa niederkniend*) Sapperlot Ich bin todt Vor Entzücken bin ich todt!	**PINTO** (*kneeling before Clarissa in a voice breaking with emotion*) The dickens I am dead, thrilled to death!
AMBROSIO (*bei Seite und wie im 1. Akt parodierend*) Steh'n Sie auf, Sie loser Mann!	**AMBROSIO** (*aside and parodying as in the first act*) Stand up, you poor man!
CLARISSA UND LAURA Was beginnt er? Was ersinnt er? Was, verliert er Den Verstand?	**CLARISSA AND LAURA** What's he beginning? What's he contriving? What, has he lost his reason?
GOMEZ Hat er den Verstand verloren? Kaum bezähm' ich meinen Zorn!	**GOMEZ** Has he gone crazy? I can hardly restrain my anger!
PANTALEONE Was thut der arme Tropf? Was spukt in seinem Kopf?	**PANTALEONE** What's the poor fellow doing? What is going on in his head?
PINTO (*steht langsam und verdutzt auf*)	**PINTO** (*gets up slowly and confusedly*)
GASTON UND AMBROSIO Haha, Pinto!	**GASTON AND AMBROSIO** Haha, Pinto!
CHOR Den Verstand will er verlieren! Vor Entzücken ist er todt, (*neckend*) Aber Pinto, armer Pinto! Armer Pinto de Fonseca!	**CHORUS** He will lose his reason! He will die from ecstasy! (*turning*) But Pinto, poor Pinto! Poor Pinto de Fonseca!
PINTO (*der immer ängstlicher geworden ist und am ganzen Leibe zu zittern beginnt, mit bebender Stimme*) Holde Schöne! Soll mich gleich der Teufel holen, Mache ich mich auf die Sohlen Ehe mich der Teufel hole!	**PINTO** (*who becomes ever more worried and who is starting to shake with a catch in his voice*) Lovely beauty! The devil shall take me! I'm getting out of here before the devil takes me!

AMBROSIO
(*höhnend bei Seite*)
Ach, das klingt doch gar zu herrlich!

PINTO
(*sich den Schweiß abwischend*)
Gott, das ist doch zu beschwerlich!

GOMEZ
(*zornig*)
Nun ist's genug, nun ist's genug!
Jetzt mach' ich ein End dem tollen Tag!

GASTON
(*in größter Heiterkeit bei Seite*)
Immer weiter, immer weiter,
's geht recht fein, 's geht recht heiter!
Lieber kleiner, lust'ger, Pinto.
Immer zu, immer zu
Kleiner, lust'ger Pinto Du!

AMBROSIO
Seht doch den dummen Tölpel da!
Ach, er dauert mich beinah'!

GOMEZ
Jetzt ist's zu kraus
Werft ihn hinaus!

PANTALEONE
Nein, jetzt wird's zu kraus
Werft ihn hinaus!

CHOR
Nein, nun wird es doch zu kraus,
Werft den tollen Kerl hinaus!

PINTO
(*setzt sich wieder in Positur*)
Holde Schöne—
(*hält verwirrt inne und fährt dann stoßweise fort*)
Die sehr schön—
Ich bin toll—ganz vor Entzücken!
(*steigernd*)
Da Sie zuckersüßes Wesen.
(*alle überschreiend*)
Mich zu Ihrem Mann erlesen
Bitt' ich—bitt' ich—
(*mit plötzlichem Entschlusse, schreiend*)
Einen Schmatz!
(*Alles bricht in ungestüme Heiterkeit aus, ausgenommen Gomez und Pantaleone.*)

GOMEZ
(*entrüstet*)
Nein, das werd' ich nimmer dulden,
Daß ein solcher frecher Wicht
Nahen dürfte sich der Holden.
Nein, das werd' ich nimmer dulden.

AMBROSIO
(*mocking aside*)
Ah, that sounds so splendid!

PINTO
(*wiping the sweat off his brow*)
God, that is so annoying!

GOMEZ
(*angrily*)
Now that's enough, that's enough!
Now I will make an end to this crazy day!

GASTON
(*aside in great merriment*)
Go on, go on!
Things go well, things go merrily!
Dear, little, happy Pinto!
Ever so, ever so
you little, merry Pinto!

AMBROSIO
See the dumb oaf there!
Oh, I almost feel sorry for him!

GOMEZ
No, things are too confused.
Throw him out!

PANTALEONE
No, things are too confused.
Throw him out!

CHORUS
No, now things are becoming too confused,
throw out the silly knave!

PINTO
(*takes up again an arrogant posture*)
Lovely beauty—
(*stops confusedly and then continues in phrases*)
who's very beautiful—
I am crazy—totally from ecstasy!
(*getting louder*)
Since you sugar-sweet personality!
(*screaming louder than anyone*)
Picked me to be your husband,
I ask—I ask—
(*with sudden resolve, screaming*)
a kiss!
(*Everyone breaks out in impetuous laughter, except Gomez and Pantaleone.*)

GOMEZ
(*indignantly*)
No, I will never bear it,
that such an insolent creature
might approach the lovely one.
No, I will never bear it.

GASTON	GASTON
(*sich zornig stellend*)	(*pretending to be angry*)
Nein, das darf kein Ritter dulden,	No, no knight may bear
Daß ein solches Kalbsgesicht	that such a calf-face
Nahen dürfte sich in Hulden	may draw near in homage
Einer Dame hold und licht!	to the lady lovely and light!

PANTALEONE / PANTALEONE
(*entrüstet*) / (*indignantly*)
Nein, das darf kein Vater dulden, / No, no father can bear it.
Nein, das duld' ich nimmermehr! / No, I can never bear it!

CHOR / CHORUS
(*kichernd und flüsternd*) / (*giggling and whispering*)
Welch' ein Pinto, was ein Pinto! / What a Pinto! What a Pinto!
Welch' ein dicker, lust'ger Pinto! / What a fat, merry Pinto!
Den Verstand will er verlieren, / He wants to lose his reason,
Ei, wo mag er ihn nur spüren? / oh, where might he keep it?
Seht das Kalbsgesicht! / See the calf-face!

CLARISSA / CLARISSA
Oh, welch' ein seltsam Abenteuer! / Oh, what a strange adventure!
Welch tolles Wesen treibt hier Spott? / What a crazy character comes here to make fun?
Kaum kann ich's tragen, großer Gott! / I can hardly bear it, great God!

LAURA / LAURA
Ei, wär' mir ein netter Anverlobter! / Oh, that would be a fine fiancé for me!
Käm' zu mir ein solcher Freier schlank, / If such a suitor came to me as a lanky one,
So würd' ich's sagen: "Schöner Jünker, vielen Dank!" / I would say: "Handsome nobleman, many thanks!"

GASTON / GASTON
(*bei Seite*) / (*aside*)
Dieser Spaß ist zum Entzücken / This joke is delightful,
Niemals könnt' er besser glücken! / never could it have turned out better!
Dank Dir, Pinto, Kalbsgesicht! / Thank you, Pinto, calf-face!
Das vergesse ich Dir nicht! / I will not forget that!
O theurer Pinto, meinen Dank, / O priceless Pinto, my thanks,
Dir vergess' ich nicht! / I will not forget your part in this!

GOMEZ / GOMEZ
Nein, nicht länger will ich's tragen! / No, I can bear it no longer!
Ist erhört ein solch' Betragen? / Have you ever heard of such behavior?
Nein, das duld' ich länger nicht, / No, I can bear it no longer!
Fort, hinaus, Du frecher Wicht! / Away, out, you insolent creature!

AMBROSIO / AMBROSIO
(*bei Seite*) / (*aside*)
Dieser Spaß ist zum Entzücken / This joke is delightful,
Doch ist's Zeit sich bald zu drücken! / but now it's time to move along!
Denn ein Kluger denkt an's Ende / A wise man calls it quits
Ehe sich die Sache wende! / before something goes awry!

PANTALEONE / PANTALEONE
Nun hab' ich satt die tollen Possen, / Now I've had enough of crazy tricks,
Längst schon hat es mich verdrossen! / I have been annoyed for a good while!
Du Narr, fort, hinaus denn! / You fool, away, out then!

CHOR / CHORUS
Nun fort, hinaus Du toller Narr! / Now out, away, you crazy fool!

PINTO
(*flehend, voller Angst*)
Ich bin Pinto de Fonseca
Und ich suche meine Braut!

CHOR
(*nachäffend*)
—und ich suche meine Braut!
Suche, Pinto!

PINTO
Ich bin Pinto!
(*Er erblickt Gaston und fährt auf diesen los.*)
Dieser hier kann's mir bezeugen,
Dieser ist an allem Schuld!
(*ganz außer sich schreiend*)
O Du Räuber, Dieb, Betrüger!
O Du schnöder Wegelag'rer!

CHOR
Ei, was ficht den dummen
Tölpel doch nur an?
Aber Pinto, kleiner Pinto, sag',
Wo hast du deine Braut?

GASTON
(*sich zornig stellend*)
Herr, jetzt zieht Euren Degen
Meine Schmach tilgt Euer Blut!
Raus den Degen, seid auf der Hut
Sonst fallet Ihr sofort meiner Wuth!

CHOR
Herr, jetzt zieht Euren Degen,
Diesen Schimpf sühnt Euer Blut!
Fliess' es hin in rothen Strömen
Nehmt zusammen Euern Muth!
Seht, wie Gaston zürnt, deswegen
Nehmt zusammen Euern Muth!

PANTALEONE, AMBROSIO, GOMEZ, CLARISSA,
UND LAURA
Zieht den Degen, närrischer Wicht!

PINTO
(*ängstlich*)
Ich den Degen? Nein!
Nein doch, laßt das sein!

GASTON
Zieht den Degen, zieht den Degen
Diesen Schimpf sühnt Euer Blut!

CHOR
Herr, jetzt zieht Euren Degen,
Ja, jetzt braucht er seinen Muth!
Jetzt fliesst Euer Bluth!

PINTO
(*beseeching, full of fear*)
I am Pinto de Fonseca
and I seek my bride!

CHORUS
(*aping him*)
—and I seek my bride!
Seek, Pinto!

PINTO
I am Pinto!
(*He looks at Gaston and flares up.*)
This one can attest to me,
since it's all his fault!
(*screaming beside himself*)
Oh, you robber, thief, betrayer!
Oh, you contemptuous highwayman!

CHORUS
Oh, what possesses
the dumb fool?
But, Pinto, little Pinto, say,
where is your bride?

GASTON
(*pretending to be angry*)
Sir, now pull your sword—
your blood will wash away my shame!
Out with the sword! Be careful
so that you don't fall victim to my fury!

CHORUS
Sir, now pull your sword,
this outrage demands your blood!
May it flow in red streams!
Gather your courage together!
See, how Gaston fumes, so
pull together your courage!

PANTALEONE, AMBROSIO, GOMEZ, CLARISSA,
AND LAURA
Draw the sword, foolish creature!

PINTO
(*nervously*)
I, the sword? No!
Not yet, let it be!

GASTON
Draw the sword, draw the sword
this outrage demands your blood!

CHORUS
Sir, now draw your sword,
yes, now he needs his courage!
Now your blood will flow!

CLARISSA Schonet, schonet sein, Herr Ritter, Seht den Ärmsten, wie er bebt!	**CLARISSA** Spare him, spare him sir knight, see the poor one, how he shakes!
GASTON (*herausfordend*) Zieht den Degen! Sonst stoße ich Euch nieder, Wie man einen Hasen spießt!	**GASTON** (*in a challenging voice*) Draw the sword! Otherwise I will knock you down, as you spear a rabbit!
PINTO Heil'ger Gott! Wie einen Hasen! Einen Hasen, wehe, wehe! Steckt den Degen ein, Herr Ritter! Steckt doch Euren Degen! Guter Ritter, thut mir nichts!	**PINTO** Holy God! Like a rabbit! A rabbit, alas, alas! Sheathe the sword, sir knight! Sheathe your sword! Good knight, don't hurt me!
CHOR Seht doch den Wicht! Schämt er sich nicht! Jammergestalt! Wirst Du nun bald Fort aus dem Staube Dich machen, Du Jammergestalt? Fort, hinaus, Du feiger Wicht!	**CHORUS** See the creature! Isn't he ashamed! A picture of misery! Will you make tracks away from here you picture of misery? Away, out, you cowardly creature!
PANTALEONE Pfui des Feiglings!	**PANTALEONE** Phooey on the coward!
GOMEZ Pfui des Feiglings!	**GOMEZ** Phooey on the coward!
GASTON Fort, hinaus, Du feiger Wicht!	**GASTON** Out, away, you cowardly creature!
ALLE Niemals laß Dich wiederseh'n!	**ALL** Never to see you again!
PINTO Ach, ich will ja gerne gehen Nie sollt Ihr mich wiederseh'n!	**PINTO** Oh, I will gladly leave, and you will never see me again!
CLARISSA, LAURA, GOMEZ Fort, hinaus! Fort, hinaus!	**CLARISSA, LAURA, GOMEZ** Out, away! Out, away!
ALLE Gehe, geh', dieses ist der Ehre Haus!	**ALL** Go, go, this is a house of honor!
AMBROSIO UND CHOR (*umdrängen Pinto*) Fort mit Pinto! Fort, hinaus! Dieses ist der Ehre Haus! Fahre ab, Du feiger Wicht, Fort, hinaus, Du Kalbsgesicht! (*Pinto wird hinausgeworfen.*) Fort, Don Pinto!	**AMBROSIO AND CHORUS** (*surrounding Pinto*) Away with Pinto! Away, out! This is a house of honor! Get out, you cowardly creature, away, out, you calf-face! (*Pinto is thrown out.*) Away, Don Pinto!

Scene 8

Die Vorigen ohne Pinto

DIALOG

CLARISSA
(*zu Gomez*) O Gott, welch' sonderbares Ereignis!

GOMEZ
(*zu Clarissa*) Auch ich bin gar befremdet!

PANTALEONE
Sah man je einen so tollen Burschen! Ein solcher feiger Schuft will ein Fonseca sein! (*zu Gomez*) Die Feigheit, wahrlich, ist in Eurem Stamme nicht bekannt, edler Don Pinto! Fonsecas sind alle Helden—gleich den Pachecos!

GOMEZ
(*leise zu Clarissa*) O Geliebte, kaum trag' ich's länger! Welch ein Betrug!

GASTON
(*zu Pantaleone*) Und dennoch, Don Pantaleone, war jener Feigling ein Fonseca!

PANTALEONE
Was sagt Ihr, Herr! Don Pinto, duldet Ihr die Schmach?

GASTON
Ich aber wiederhole es Euch, er war ein Fonseca, ja mehr noch, er ist Don Pinto de Fonseca!

ALLE
Don Pinto de Fonseca?

GOMEZ
(*zu Gaston*) So triebt Ihr Euer Spiel mit mir? Ihr seid nicht Don Pinto?

GASTON
Ich bin Don Gaston de Viratos!

GOMEZ
Das sollt Ihr büßen! (*Er greift zum Degen.*)

GASTON
Laßt stecken, Don Gomez!

PANTALEONE
Wie?—Don Gomez?

GOMEZ
Ja denn, edler Herr, ich bin Don Gomez de Freiros.

PANTALEONE
Don Gomez de Freiros—schändlicher Betrug! Das büßt Ihr mir!

Scene 8

As before, but without Pinto

DIALOGUE

CLARISSA
(*to Gomez*) Oh God, what a strange turn of events!

GOMEZ
(*to Clarissa*) I'm also astonished!

PANTALEONE
Have you ever seen such a crazy chap! Such a cowardly rascal wants to be a Fonseca! (*to Gomez*) The cowardice, is truly unknown in your family tree, noble Don Pinto! All the Fonsecas are heroes—like the Pachecos!

GOMEZ
(*softly to Clarissa*) Oh, beloved, I can hardly bear it any longer! What a fraud!

GASTON
(*to Pantaleone*) And yet, Don Pantaleone, that coward was a Fonseca!

PANTALEONE
What do you say, sir! Don Pinto, can you bear such dishonor?

GASTON
I tell you again, he was a Fonseca, moreover, he is Don Pinto de Fonseca!

ALL
Don Pinto de Fonseca?

GOMEZ
(*to Gaston*) So you had your fun with me? You are not Don Pinto?

GASTON
I am Don Gaston de Viratos!

GOMEZ
You will pay for that! (*He is about to pull out his sword.*)

GASTON
Let it alone, Don Gomez!

PANTALEONE
What—Don Gomez?

GOMEZ
Yes, noble sir, I am Don Gomez de Freiros.

PANTLEONE
Don Gomez de Freiros—a shameful fraud! You will pay for that!

CLARISSA
(*sich dazwischen werfend*) Um aller Heiligen willen! Vater, ich liebe ihn—mehr als mein Leben! Erst tötet mich—

GASTON
Ei, edle Herren, welche Verblendung! (*zu Pantaleone*) Ihr, Don Pantaleone, gewannt, statt eines blöden Feiglings, einen tapferen, ritterlichen Eidam aus Spaniens edelstem Geschlecht, für Eure Tochter den Geliebten. (*zu Gomez*) Ihr, Herr, gewannt Euer Lebensglück und zürnt mir, daß ich nicht Don Pinto bin! Ihr solltet Dank mir wissen, daß mein toller Streich Euch so leichten Kaufs von dem wahren Don Pinto befreit!

GOMEZ
Verzeiht, Don Gaston, meine Heftigkeit—

CLARISSA
Wie dank ich Euch, Don Gaston! (*Gomez und Clarissa werfen sich vor Don Pantaleone nieder.*) Könnt Ihr verzeihen, teurer Vater? Seht, unser höchstes Glück liegt nun in Euer Hand!

GASTON
(*zu Pantaleone*) Zieht den Vergleich—und sagt noch nein!

PANTALEONE
(*grollend*) Ihr Betrüger!

GASTON
Nur eine List gegen Eure Laune!

PANTALEONE
(*auffahrend*) Eine Laune?

GASTON
Nichts als eine Laune! Bedenkt, wohin sie führen konnte—Eurer Tochter Unglück—Eure Reue—

PANTALEONE
(*nach einigem Besinnen*) Nun denn, so sei's! Don Gomez, Euer Geschlecht ist reich an Ehren.

GASTON
(*einfallend*) Reich an Geld und Gut—

PANTALEONE
Ihr seid von edlem Anstand—aus Euren Zügen spricht ein kühner, stolzer Geist—

CLARISSA
Und Vater, ach, ich liebe ihn so sehr!

PANTALEONE
So seid mir, denn als Eidam an Pintos Statt willkommen!

GOMEZ UND CLARISSA
(*springen auf und umarmen ihn*) Vater, Vater!

CLARISSA
(*throws herself between them*) By all the saints! Father, I love him—more than my own life! Kill me first—

GASTON
Oh, noble sirs, what confusion! (*to Pantaleone*) You, Don Pantaleone, win instead of a stupid coward, a brave, knightly son-in-law from Spain's noblest family as the beloved of your daughter. (*to Gomez*) You, sir, won your life's happiness and storm at me for not being Don Pinto! You should know, that thanks to my crazy prank, you are freed from the true Don Pinto very easily.

GOMEZ
Don Gaston, forgive my vehemence—

CLARISSA
I thank you with all my heart, Don Gaston! (*Gomez and Clarissa throw themselves in front of Don Pantaleone.*) Can you forgive us, dear father? See, our greatest happiness now lies in your hands!

GASTON
(*to Pantaleone*) Make a comparison—and then say no!

PANTALEONE
(*grumbling*) You deceivers!

GASTON
Only a strategy against your mood!

PANTALEONE
(*flaring up*) A mood?

GASTON
Nothing but a mood! Consider where it could have led—To your daughter's misfortune—to your remorse—

PANTALEONE
(*after some reflection*) Now then, so be it! Don Gomez, your family is blessed with honor!

GASTON
(*interrupting him*) Blessed with money and goods—

PANTALEONE
You are of noble breeding—your face shows a bold, proud mind—

CLARISSA
And, father, oh, I love him so very much!

PANTALEONE
So be welcome, then, as son-in-law in Pinto's stead!

GOMEZ AND CLARISSA
(*jump up and hug him*) Father, father!

(Gaston und Ambrosio treten bei Seite, während Pantaleone, Gomez, Clarissa, und Laura händeschüttelnd und glückwünschend beisammen stehen.)

No. 21. Finale B

CHOR DER MÄNNER
Heil sei Euch, Don Pantaleone,
Heil der Tochter, Heil dem Sohne,
Den die Liebe Euch geschenkt!
Preis der Weisheit, Preis der Milde,
Die dem alten Wappenschilde
Glanz und Pracht auf's Neu' verlieh'n!

GASTON
(*zu Ambrosio*)
Nun, was sagst Du, Don Ambrosio,
Dacht'st Du Dir die Sache auch so?
Alles scheint im rechten Geleis!

AMBROSIO
Nun, Herr Ritter, meinetwegen!
Da wir nichts gewinnen konnten
Scheint mir wenig d'ran gelegen,
Wer die Braut von dannen führte!

CHOR DER FRAUEN
Möcht' es Jeder doch gelingen
Den Geliebten zu erringen
Durch der Liebe heil'ge Mächte!
Mög' sie mit des Vaters Segen
Allem Schicksalstrotz entgegen
Ein zum Glück der Ehe geh'n!

GASTON
(*tritt an das Brautpaar heran*)
Schöne Donna, edler Ritter, meinen
Glück und Segenswunsch!

CHOR
Heil, edles Paar!

AMBROSIO
(*der ebenfalls herangetreten*)
Hier auf Eurem Hochzeitsschmause
Da will ich recht lustig springen!

LAURA
(*zu Clarissa*)
Hochzeit, Hochzeit! lustig, lustig!

GASTON
(*zu Gomez*)
Hochzeit, Hochzeit! lustig, lustig!

PANTALEONE
Ei, wie lustig!

CHOR
Lustig springen, lustig springen!

(Gaston and Ambrosio step to the side, while Pantaleone, Gomez, Clarissa, and Laura stay shaking hands and wishing each other good luck.)

No. 21. Finale B

MEN'S CHORUS
Hail to you, Don Pantaleone,
hail to the daughter, hail to the son,
whom Love gave to you!
Praise to wisdom, praise to kindness,
which lend the old coat-of-arms
brightness and splendor anew!

GASTON
(*to Ambrosio*)
Now what do you say, Don Ambrosio,
do you think it would end this way?
Everything appears to work out!

AMBROSIO
Now, sir knight, as you like it!
Since we could not win anything,
it appears to me of little importance
who takes the bride!

WOMEN'S CHORUS
May each one succeed
to win her beloved
through the blessed powers of Love!
May she, with the father's blessing
approach the happiness of marriage
against the impediment of fate!

GASTON
(*approaches the bridal couple*)
Beautiful lady, noble knight,
I wish you happiness and blessings!

CHORUS
Hail, noble couple!

AMBROSIO
(*who likewise steps forward*)
Here at your wedding feast
will I dance merrily!

LAURA
(*to Clarissa*)
Marriage, marriage! Joy, joy!

GASTON
(*to Gomez*)
Marriage, marriage! Joy, joy!

PANTALEONE
Oh, how merry!

CHORUS
Dance merrily! Dance merrily!

AMBROSIO
Kastagnetten hör' ich klingen:
Dumm trrrum, dumm trrrum!
Flöt und Clarinetten singen:
Dudeldideldia! Dudeldideldia!

CLARISSA
(*zu Gomez*)
Ewig nun die Deine!

GOMEZ
(*zu Clarissa*)
Jetzt halt ich Dich auf ewig!

LAURA
Das wird ein Spaß!
Wie will ich tanzen und springen!
Heißa! Heißa! wie noch nie!

GASTON
Der Bursch ist toll, ist ganz närrisch!
(*zu Ambrosio*)
Recht so, recht so!

PANTALEONE
Ei, seht doch,
Solche Sachen
Sind zum Lachen!

GOMEZ
Clarissa—und alsdann—!

CLARISSA
Seligkeit!

CHOR DER FRAUEN
Selige Liebe!

CHOR DER MÄNNER
Höchste Freude!

GOMEZ UND CLARISSA
Ja, Seligkeit!

LAURA
O schönster Tag!

GASTON UND AMBROSIO
Das dankt Ihr nun Don Pinto!

ALLGEMEINER CHOR
Nun des Lebens Freud' entgegen!
Jeder Tag bringt neuen Segen,
Vorwärts auf des Glückes Spur!
Seht, Euch winken süße Wonnen,
Zukunft steht voll lichter Sonnen,
Selig lacht die Gegenwart!

ENDE

AMBROSIO
I hear castanettes ringing:
Dumm trrrum, dumm trrrum!
Flutes and clarinets are singing:
Dudeldideldia! Dudeldideldia!

CLARISSA
(*to Gomez*)
I am forever yours!

GOMEZ
(*to Clarissa*)
Now I hold you forever!

LAURA
That will be fun!
How I will dance and leap!
Huzzah, huzzah! As never before!

GASTON
The boy is crazy, is entirely foolish!
(*to Ambrosio*)
Right so, right so!

PANTALEONE
Oh, see,
such things
make one laugh out loud!

GOMEZ
Clarissa—and then—!

CLARISSA
Bliss!

WOMEN'S CHORUS
Holy love!

MEN'S CHORUS
Highest joy!

GOMEZ AND CLARISSA
Yes, bliss!

LAURA
Oh, most beautiful day!

GASTON AND AMBORSIO
That you owe to Don Pinto!

MIXED CHORUS
Now face the joy of life!
Each day brings new blessings,
forward on the path of happiness!
See, sweet delights beckon,
the future stands full of bright suns,
the present smiles happily!

END

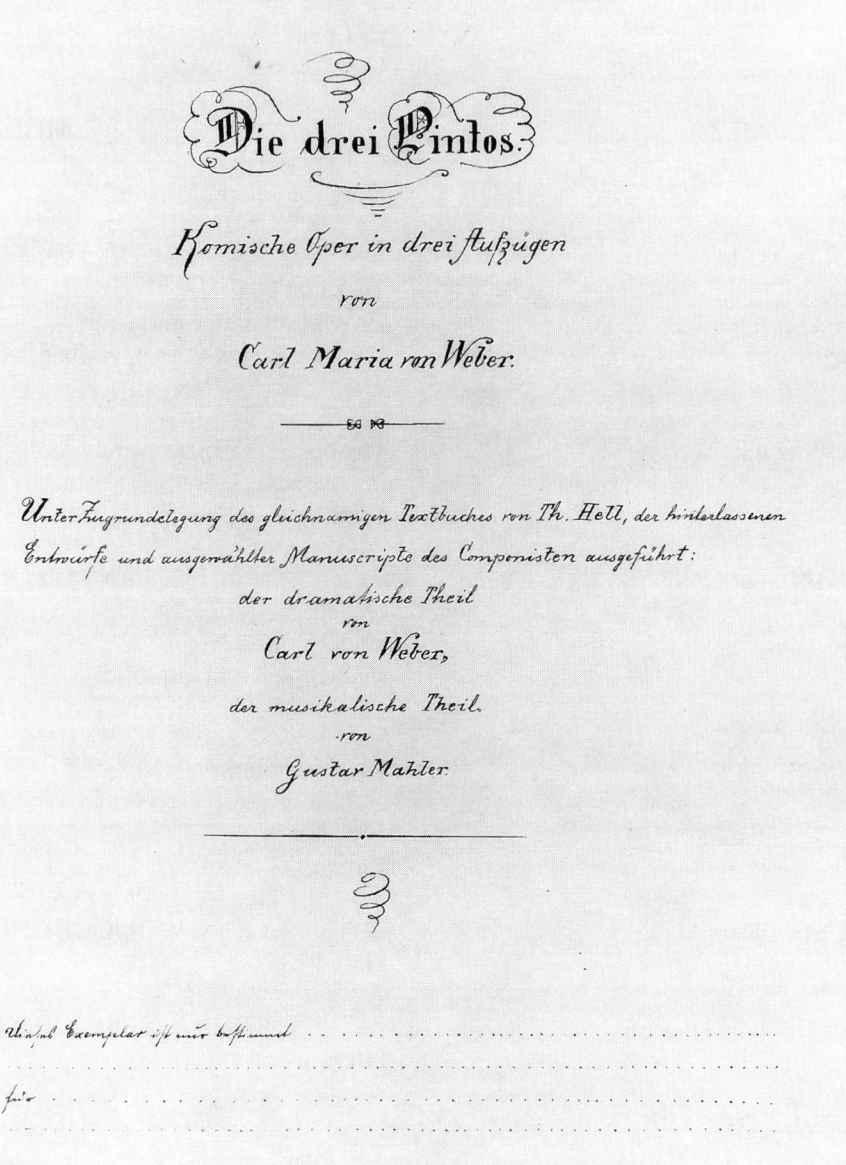

Plate 1. Carl Maria von Weber, *Die drei Pintos: Komische Oper in drei Aufzügen,* der dramatische Theil von Carl von Weber, der musikalische Theil von Gustav Mahler (Leipzig: C. F. Kahnt, [1888]), ed. no. 2953, title page. Lithograph of the copyists' score. Courtesy of Bibliothèque musicale Gustav Mahler, Paris.

Plate 2. *Die drei Pintos*, beginning of no. 1, Ensemble, "Leeret die Becher." Lithograph of the copyists' score. Courtesy of Bibliothèque musicale Gustav Mahler, Paris.

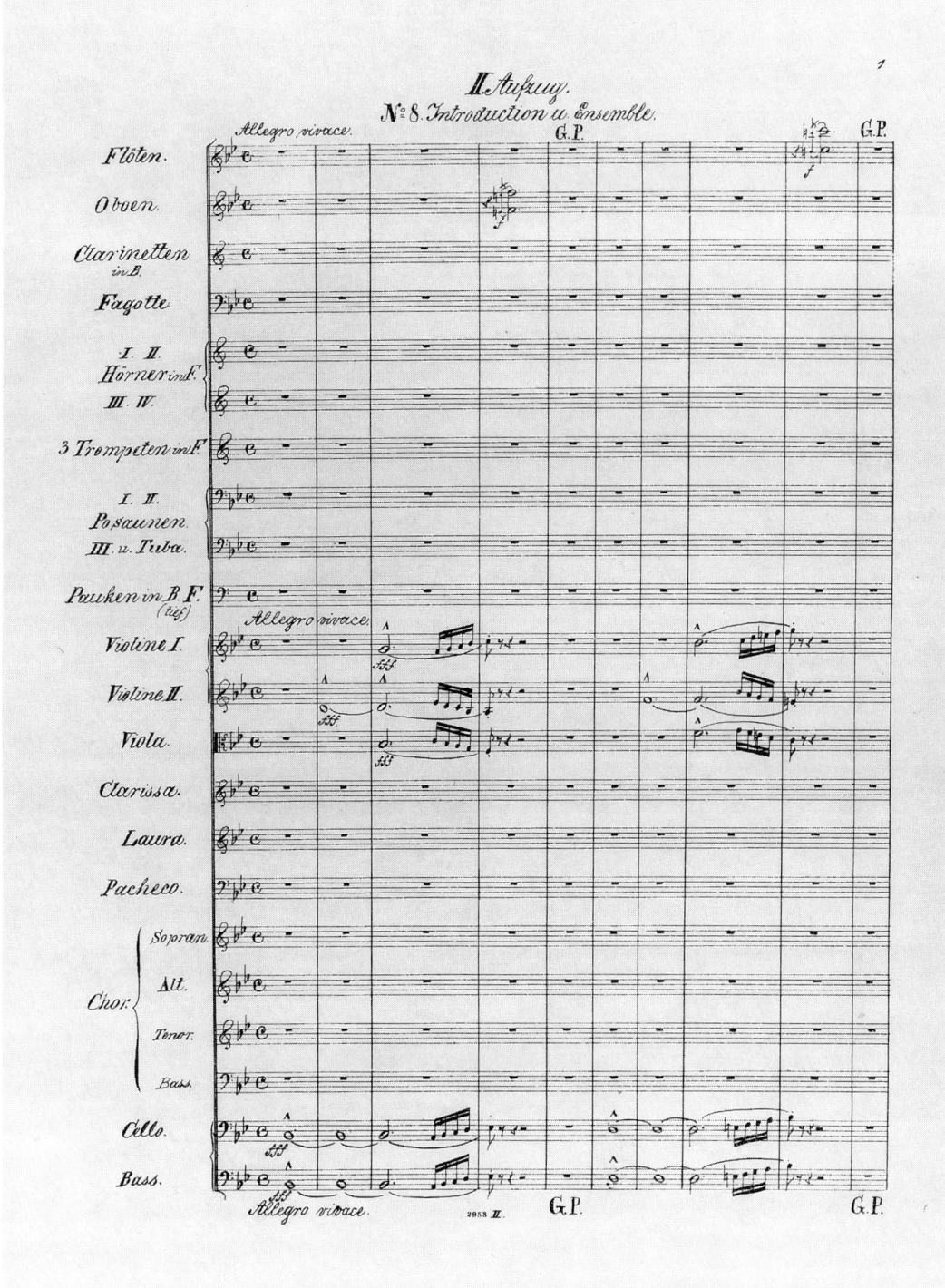

Plate 3. *Die drei Pintos*, beginning of no. 8, Introduction und Ensemble, "Wißt Ihr nicht, was wir hier sollen?" Lithograph of the copyists' score. Courtesy of Bibliothèque musicale Gustav Mahler, Paris.

Plate 4. C. M. von Weber, *Die drei Pintos: Komische Oper in drei Aufzügen*, der dramatische Theil von C. von Weber, der musikalische von G. Mahler, Klavier-Auszug mit Text (Leipzig: C. F. Kahnt, [1888]), ed. no. 1455, title page. Courtesy of Bibliothèque musicale Gustav Mahler, Paris.

Die drei Pintos

Komische Oper in drei Aufzügen

PERSONEN

Don Pantaleone Roiz de Pacheco ⎫
Don Gomez Freiros ⎬ Edelleute zu Madrid
Clarissa, Don Pantaleone's Tochter
Laura, Clarissen's Zofe
Don Gaston Viratos, ehemals Student zu Salamanca

Don Pinto de Fonseca, ein junger Landedelmann aus Castilla
Der Wirth der Dorfschänke zu Peñaranda
Inez, dessen Tochter
Ambrosio, Don Gaston's Diener
Der Haushofmeister Don Pantaleone's
Studenten von Salamanca
Dienerschaft im Hause des Don Pantaleone und in der Dorfschänke zu Peñaranda

CHARACTERS

Don Pantaleone Roiz de Pacheco [bass] ⎫
Don Gomez Freiros [tenor] ⎬ Nobles of Madrid
Clarissa, Don Pantaleone's daughter [soprano]
Laura, Clarissa's maid [mezzo-soprano]
Don Gaston Viratos, erstwhile student at Salamanca [tenor]

Don Pinto de Fonseca, a young country squire from Castille [bass]
The Innkeeper of the village inn at Peñaranda [bass]
Inez, his daughter [soprano]
Ambrosio, Don Gaston's servant [baritone]
The Steward of Don Pantaleone [tenor]
Students from Salamanca [chorus]
Servants in the house of Don Pantaleone and in the village inn at Peñaranda [chorus]

INSTRUMENTS

Piccolo (Picc.) 1, 2
Flute (Fl.) 1, 2
Oboe (Ob.) 1, 2
Clarinet (Cl.) 1, 2
Bassoon (Bn.) 1, 2
Horn (Hn.) 1, 2
Horn (Hn.) 3, 4
Trumpet (Tpt.) 1, 2
Trumpet (Tpt.) 3
Trombone (Trb.) 1, 2
Trombone (Trb.) 3
Tuba (Tb.)

Timpani (Timp.)
Cymbals (Cym.)
Bass Drum (B. Drum)
Triangle (Trgl.)
Tambourine (Tamb.)
Castanets (Cast.)
Ruthe (Ruthe)
Violin (Vn.) 1
Violin (Vn.) 2
Viola (Va.)
Violoncello (Vc.)
Contrabass (Cb.)

I. Aufzug
No. 1. Ensemble

5
Fl. 1, 2
a 2
Ob. 1, 2
a 2
Cl. 1, 2
a 2
Bn. 1, 2
a 2
a 2
Hn. 1, 2
fff
Hn. 3, 4
fff
Tpt. 1, 2
Timp.
Vn. 1
f
Vn. 2
f
Va.
f
Vc.
Cb.

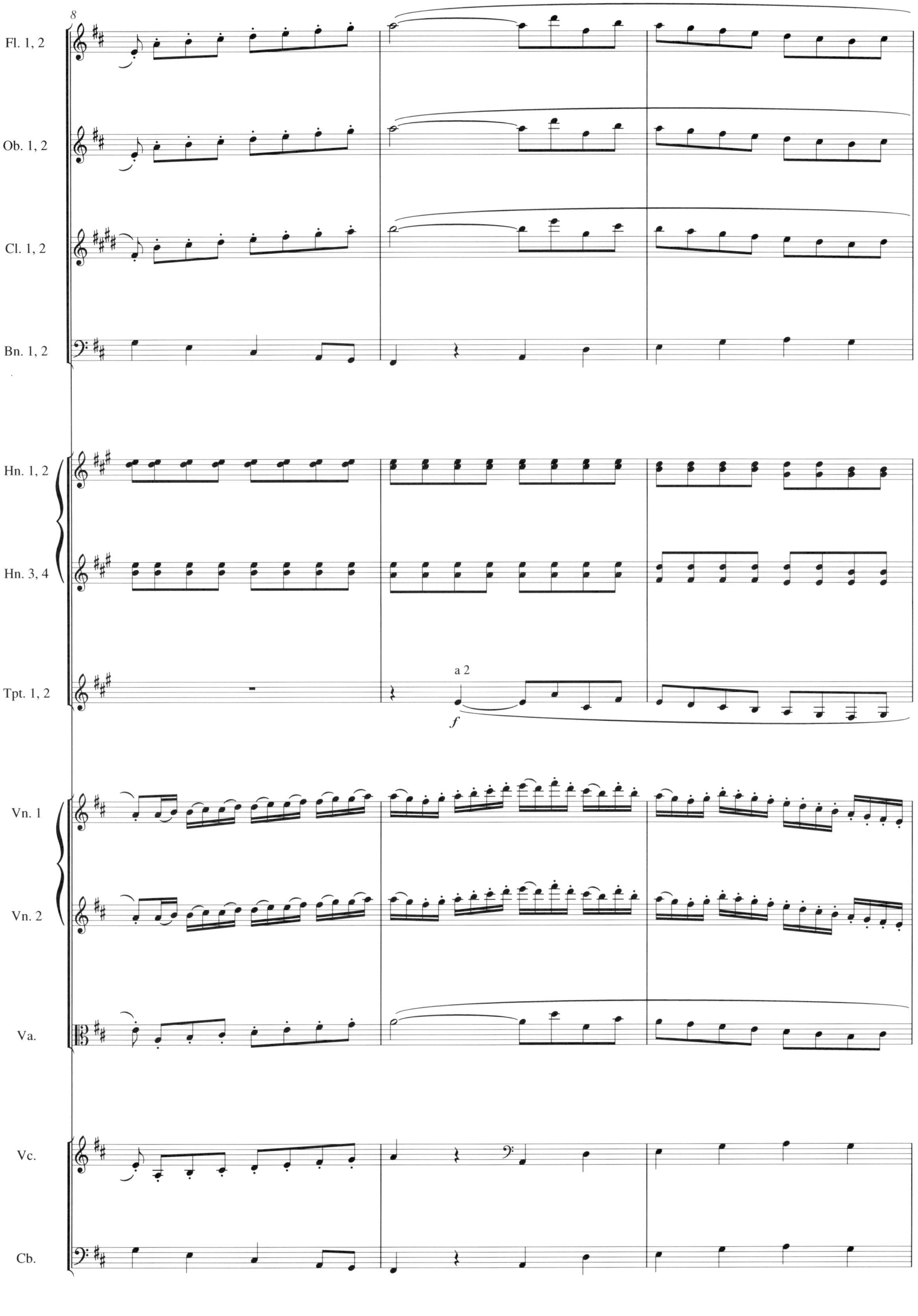
8
Fl. 1, 2
Ob. 1, 2
Cl. 1, 2
Bn. 1, 2
Hn. 1, 2
Hn. 3, 4
Tpt. 1, 2
a 2
f
Vn. 1
Vn. 2
Va.
Vc.
Cb.

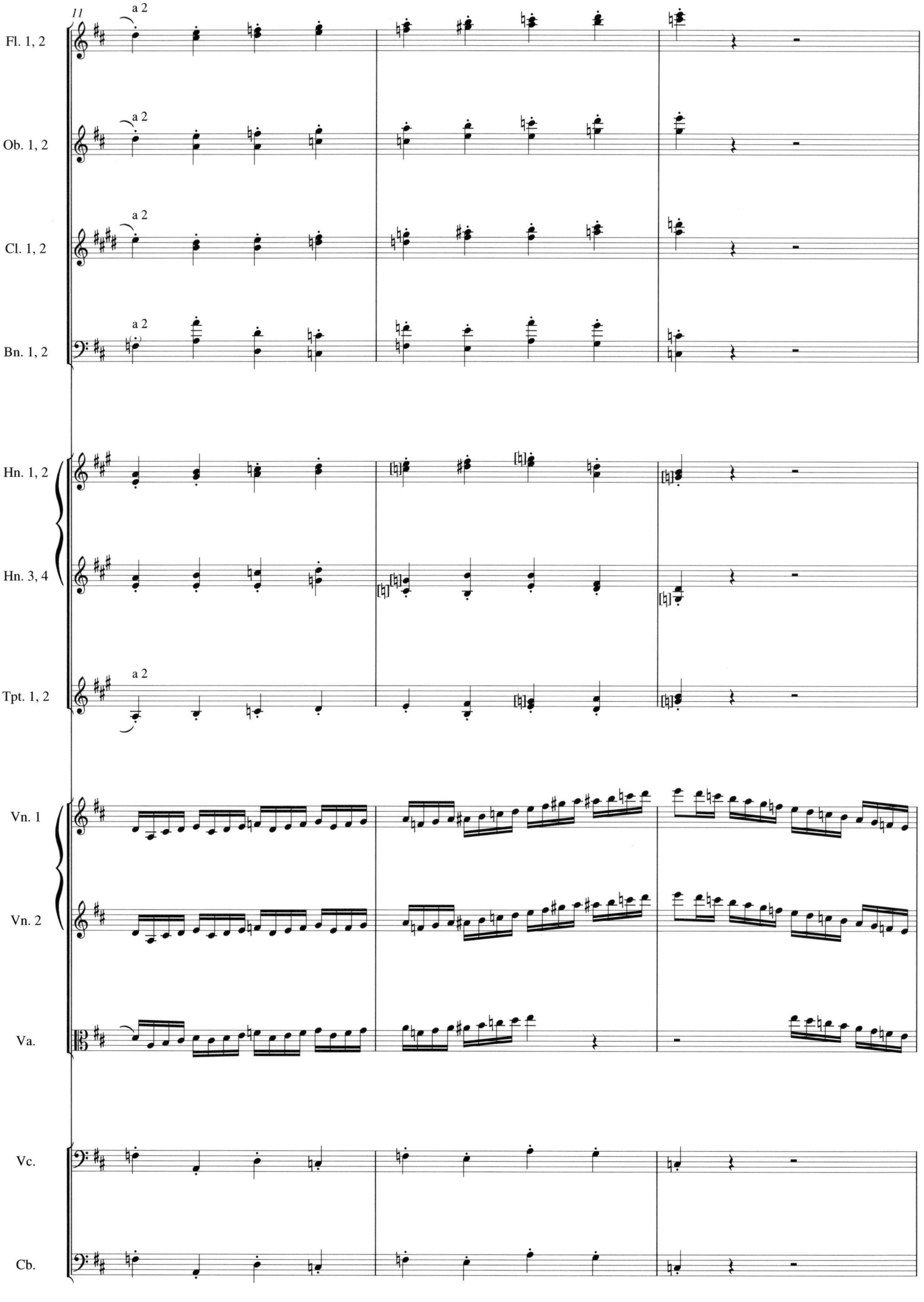
11
a 2
Fl. 1, 2
Ob. 1, 2
Cl. 1, 2
Bn. 1, 2
Hn. 1, 2
Hn. 3, 4
Tpt. 1, 2
Vn. 1
Vn. 2
Va.
Vc.
Cb.

7

A
Vorhang auf
a 2
tr
17
Fl. 1, 2
Ob. 1, 2
Cl. 1, 2
Bn. 1, 2
Hn. 1, 2
Hn. 3, 4
Tpt. 1, 2
Timp.
p
cresc.
Vn. 1
Vn. 2
Va.
Vc.
Cb.
Vorhang auf

20
Fl. 1, 2
Ob. 1, 2
Cl. 1, 2
Bn. 1, 2
Hn. 1, 2
Hn. 3, 4
Timp.
Vn. 1
Vn. 2
STUDENTEN-CHOR
T1
Lee- ret die
T2
Lee- ret die
B1
Lee- ret die
B2
Lee- ret die
Vc.
Cb.

23
a 2
Fl. 1, 2
a 2
Ob. 1, 2
a 2
Cl. 1, 2
Bn. 1, 2
mf
Hn. 1, 2
mf
f
a 2
Hn. 3, 4
mf
f
in A-E
Timp.
ff
Vn. 1
mf
Vn. 2
mf
T1
Be- cher, mu- ti- ge Ze- cher, bis auf den
T2
Be- cher, mu- ti- ge Ze- cher, bis auf den
B1
Be- cher, mu- ti- ge Ze- cher, bis auf den
B2
Be- cher, mu- ti- ge Ze- cher, bis auf den
Vc.
Cb.

11

B
Etwas ruhiger
Hn. 1, 2
Hn. 3, 4
Vn. 1
Vn. 2
Va.
Gast.
T1
T2
B1
B2
Vc.
Cb.
espress.
divisi
(hervortretend)
Reicht mir den größ- ten Be- cher her, die
Nie zu ver- ges- sen,
pizz.
Ob. 1, 2
Cl. 1, 2
Bn. 1, 2
Eu- ren nehmt zu Hän- den!
Auf Sa- la- man- ca trinkt sie

13

45
C
Ob. 1, 2
Cl. 1, 2
Bn. 1, 2
a 2
Hn. 1, 2
Hn. 3, 4
Vn. 1
Vn. 2
Va.
Gast.
SOLO-STUDENT [GASTON]
Auf e- wig bleib' sie _ frisch und grün, die
T1
-ses- sen! Sei _ heut' ge- schwo- ren!
T2
-ses- sen! Sei heut' ge- schwo- ren!
B1
-ses- sen! Sei heut' ge- schwo- ren!
B2
-ses- sen! Sei heut' ge- schwo- ren!
Vc.
Cb.

Ju- gendkraft, die Jugendkraft, die alles kühne Streben zum höchsten, höch-sten Ziel, zum höch- sten Ziel _____ muß he- ben! Auf

Auf

Auf

e-wig bleib' sie frisch und grün, die Jugendkraft, die Jugendkraft, des

64
Ob. 1, 2
a 2
Cl. 1, 2
Bn. 1, 2
a 2
Hn. 1, 2
Hn. 3, 4
Tpt. 1, 2
[1]
Trb. 1, 2
mf
Trb. 3
Tb.
mf
Vn. 1
mf
Vn. 2
mf
Va.
mf
Gast.
Her- zens kühn- stes Stre- ben! Auf zum höch- sten, höch- sten,
T1
Her- zens kühn- stes Stre- ben! Auf zum höch- sten, höch- sten
höch- sten Ziel, zum
T2
Her- zens kühn- stes Stre- ben! Auf zum höch- sten, höch- sten
höch- sten Ziel, zum
B1
Her- zens kühn- stes Stre- ben! Auf zum höch- sten, höch- sten
höch- sten Ziel, zum
B2
Her- zens kühn- stes Stre- ben! Auf zum höch- sten, höch- sten
höch- sten Ziel, zum
Vc.
arco
mf
Cb.
arco
mf

68
E
a 2
Fl. 1, 2
Ob. 1, 2
Cl. 1, 2
Bn. 1, 2
Hn. 1, 2
Hn. 3, 4
Tpt. 1, 2
Trb. 1, 2
Trb. 3
Tb.
Vn. 1
Vn. 2
Va.
col legno
sempre cresc.
Gast.
höch- sten, höch- sten Ziel! Die
T1
T2
Ziel, zum höch- sten Ziel! Die
B1
B2
Ziel, zum höch- sten Ziel! Die
T1
T2
höch- sten Ziel! La, la, la, la, la, la, la, la, la, la, la, la,
B1
B2
höch- sten Ziel! La, la, la, la, la, la, la, la, la, la, la, la,
Vc.
Cb.

72
a 2
Ob. 1, 2
cresc.
Cl. 1, 2
cresc.
Bn. 1, 2
Hn. 1, 2
Hn. 3, 4
cresc.
Tpt. 1, 2
Tpt. 3
Vn. 1
cresc.
natürlich
Vn. 2
cresc.
natürlich
Va.
cresc.
natürlich
Gast.
Ju- gend-kraft, die Ju- gend-kraft, die Ju- gend- kraft! Las-set die
T1 T2
cresc.
Ju- gend-kraft, die Ju- gend-kraft, die Ju- gend- kraft! Las-set die
B1 B2
[cresc.]
Ju- gend-kraft, die Ju- gend-kraft, die Ju- gend- kraft! Las-set die
T1 T2
la, la, la, la, la, la, la, la, la, la, la, la, la, la, la, la, la, die Ju- gend- kraft! Las-set die
B1 B2
la, la, la, la, la, la, la, la, la, la, la, la, la, la, la, la, la, die Ju- gend- kraft! Las-set die
Vc.
[cresc.]
natürlich
Cb.
natürlich

Be-cher er-klin-gen, hur- rah! Sie le- be

81
L'istesso tempo
Cl. 1, 2
Bn. 1, 2
Hn. 1, 2
Hn. 3, 4
Trb. 1, 2
Trb. 3
Tb.
Timp.
L'istesso tempo
Vn. 1
Springbogen
Vn. 2
Springbogen
divisi
Va.
Springbogen
Ambr.
La, la, la, la, la, la, la, la, la, la, la, la, la, la, la, es le- be der Wein! La, la, la, la, la, la, la,
T1
T2
hoch!
B1
B2
hoch!
T1
T2
hoch!
B1
B2
hoch!
Vc.
Springbogen
Cb.
pizz.
arco
pizz.

la, la, la, la, la, la, la, la, la, es le- be das Glück!

24

25

Neu- e Freund- schaft und Lieb'!

100
F
Ruhig
Bn. 1, 2
Hn. 1, 2
p espress.
Hn. 3, 4
Ruhig
Vn. 1
Vn. 2
T1
T2
B1
B2
In- nig ver- bun- den ha- ben uns Stun- den,
104
Nachgeben!
a 2
Nachgeben!
ha- ben uns Stun- den se- lig- ster, se- lig- ster Lust!

108
G Etwas gemässigter
Cl. 1, 2
Bn. 1, 2
Hn. 1, 2
Hn. 3, 4
Vn. 1
Vn. 2
Va.
Gast.
T1
T2
B1
B2
Vc.
Cb.
p espress.
Etwas gemässigter
divisi
unis.
espress.
pizz.
Nun, Freun- de, reicht mir
Freund- schaft und Lie- be!

29

Eu- re Hand zum letz- ten Ab- schieds- gru- ße. Ich zie- he mei- nen

Weg durch's Land, Ihr kehrt zu- rück zur Mu -

119
poco rit.
Breit
Fl. 1, 2
Ob. 1, 2
Cl. 1, 2
Bn. 1, 2
a 2
Hn. 1, 2
Hn. 3, 4
p zart
Vn. 1
Vn. 2
Va.
espress.
divisi
Gast.
-se. Doch ru- fen wir voll_ Hoff- nung aus: Auf
Vc.
unis.
Cb.

Wie- der- seh'n, auf Wie- der- seh'n, mit Got- tes reich- stem Se- gen!

Heil! Heil! Heil auf al- len We-

131
J
Fl. 1, 2
Ob. 1, 2
Cl. 1, 2
a 2
p
espress.
Bn. 1, 2
Hn. 1, 2
Hn. 3, 4
Vn. 1
tr
Vn. 2
Va.
Gast.
- gen, auf _ Wie- der- seh'n!
Auf
T1
Doch ru- fen _ wir voll Hoff- nung aus: Auf
T2
Doch ru- fen _ wir voll Hoff- nung aus: Auf
B1
Auf
B2
Auf
Vc.
Cb.
pizz.

34

*Sie brechen geräuschvoll auf, ordnen sich allmählig zum Zuge und gehen, vom Gaston Abschied nehmend, nach rückwärts ab.

*(für den Regisseur) Sie schreiten in halben Takten um Gaston herum.

151
(tr)
Fl. 1
Picc.
Ob. 1, 2
Cl. 1, 2
Bn. 1, 2
a 2
ff
Hn. 1, 2
Hn. 3, 4
Tpt. 1, 2
Tpt. 3
f
Trb. 1, 2
mf
col legno
Vn. 1
Vn. 2
Va.
Gast.
auf Wie- der- seh'n, auf Wie- der-seh'n, auf
CHORUS I
T1 T2
B1 B2
CHORUS II
cresc.
p
la, la, la, la, la, la, la, la, la, la, la, la, la, la, la, la, la, la, la, la, la, la, la, la, la, la, la, la, la, auf
Vc. Cb.

38

*Gaston bleibt allein zurück.

†Hinter die Studenten in feuriger Bewegung ab. Schnellschrit.

40

41

*Hier sind die Studenten verschwunden.

43

183
Fl. 1, 2
Ob. 1, 2
Cl. 1, 2
Bn. 1, 2
Hn. 1, 2
Hn. 3, 4
Tpt. 1, 2
Timp.
Vn. 1
Vn. 2
Va.
CHORUS
T1
T2
B1
B2
(aus weiter Ferne)
Auf Wie- der-seh'n, auf Wie- der-seh'n, mit Got- tes reich- stem
Vc.
Cb.

*Gaston steht gedankenvoll an der offenen Veranda und blickt den davongehenden nach.

197
Fl. 1, 2
ppp
Ob. 1, 2
pp
ppp
Cl. 1, 2
pp
ppp
Bn. 1, 2
pp
ppp
Hn. 1, 2
pp
ppp
Vn. 1
pizz.
ppp
Vn. 2
pizz.
ppp
Va.
pizz.
ppp
T1
T2
B1
B2
Vc.
pizz.
ppp
Cb.
pizz.
ppp

No. 2. Rondo a la Polacca

Was ich dann thu', das

frag' ich mich,— frag' ich denn nicht recht wun-der-lich? Was ich dann thu', das frag' ich mich,—

frag' ich denn nicht recht wun-der-lich?

49

a 2
a tempo
Fl. 1, 2
Ob. 1, 2
Cl. 1, 2
Bn. 1, 2
Hn. 1, 2
a tempo
Vn. 1
Vn. 2
Va.
Gast.
liebt! Doch wenn sie mei-ne Hand ver-schmäht? Wenn ihr Herz nach 'nem An-dern steht?
Vc.
pizz.
Cb.
Fl. 1, 2
Ob. 1, 2
Cl. 1, 2
Bn. 1, 2
Tpt. 1, 2
Vn. 1
Vn. 2
Va.
Gast.
Wenn sie nach sprö-der Wei-ber Art fest auf ih- rem Sinn be- harrt?
Vc.
arco
Cb.

33
B
Fl. 1, 2
a 2
Ob. 1, 2
1 solo
Cl. 1, 2
Bn. 1, 2
Hn. 1, 2
Vn. 1
pizz.
Vn. 2
pizz.
Va.
pizz.
Gast.
Was ich dann thu', das frag' ich mich,—
Vc.
Cb.
37
Fl. 1, 2
[1]
Cl. 1, 2
1
Bn. 1, 2
1 solo
Vn. 1
arco
pizz.
Vn. 2
arco
pizz.
Va.
arco
arco
Gast.
frag' ich denn nicht recht wun- der- lich?
Was ich dann thu', das frag' ich _ mich!
Vc.
pizz.
arco
Cb.

rit.
C a tempo
Ob. 1, 2
Cl. 1, 2
Bn. 1, 2
Vn. 1
Vn. 2
Va.
Gast.
Vc.
Cb.
arco
[arco]
[pizz.]
pizz.
a tempo
Frag' ich denn nicht recht wun-der-lich, recht wun-der- lich?
Sprech' bei ei- ner An- dern vor,
Fl. 1, 2
Hn. 1, 2
die leiht mir ge- neig- tes _ Ohr!
Sprech' bei _ ei- ner _ An- dern vor,

50
a tempo
Fl. 1, 2
a 2
Ob. 1, 2
[1]
Cl. 1, 2
[1]
Bn. 1, 2
[1]
Hn. 1, 2
Tpt. 1, 2
Timp.
a tempo
Vn. 1
Vn. 2
Va.
Gast.
die leiht mir dann ge- neig- tes Ohr! Wahr- lich, wahr- lich, ja das thu' ich, Mäd- chen,
Vc.
[pizz.]
Cb.
[pizz.]

ei, ganz si- cher- lich! Seid Ihr nur hübsch und jung und reich,

58
Fl. 1, 2
Ob. 1, 2
Cl. 1, 2
Bn. 1, 2
Hn. 1, 2
Tpt. 1, 2
Timp.
[in E-B]
[in D-A]
Vn. 1
Vn. 2
Va.
pizz.
Gast.
seid Ihr nur hübsch und jung und reich,
seid Ihr _ vor _ mir _
Vc.
Cb.

56

ja — Al- le — gleich, ja, — ja — Al- le — gleich, d'rum, schö- ne — Mäd- chen, hü- tet Euch, d'rum, schö- ne Mäd- chen, hü- tet Euch!

No. 3. Terzettino

22
Cl. 1, 2
Bn. 1, 2
Va.
Gast.
Ambr.
Wirth
Vc.
Cb.
pp
f
[pizz.]
p hart
Geld to- tal ver- pufft! Ei, ei,
Geld to- tal ver- pufft! Ei, ei, ei, ei, ei, ei, ei, ei, ei,
Geld im Sa- che hätt'! Ei, ei,
pizz.
hart
28
[1]
ei, mein Geld to- tal ver- pufft!
ei, ei, ei, ei, ei, ei, ei, ei, ei, ei, ei, ei, ei!
ei, ei, ei, ei, ei, ei, ei! Ei!

34
B
Cl. 1, 2
Bn. 1, 2
a 2
Gast.
Ei, ei, ei, ei, ei, was liegt denn viel da- ran,
Ambr.
Ei, was liegt denn viel da- ran,
Wirth
Ei, ei, ei, da liegt mir viel da- ran,
Vc.
Cb.
43
rit.
Cl. 1, 2
Bn. 1, 2
Gast.
da- ran, was liegt denn viel da- ran!
Ambr.
da- ran, was liegt denn viel da- ran!
Wirth
da- ran, da liegt mir viel da- ran!
Vc.
Cb.

C
a tempo
Cl. 1, 2
Bn. 1, 2
Va.
arco
Gast.
Hab' ich nur gu- te Lau- ne, was kränkt mich dann das Geld!
Ambr.
Hat er nur gu- te Lau- ne, was kränkt ihn dann das Geld! Ei, ei, ei,
Wirth
Ist er bei gu- te Lau- ne, was kränkt ihn dann das Geld!
Vc.
[arco]
pizz.
Cb.
[arco]
pizz.
a 2
Bn. 1, 2
Va.
pizz.
Gast.
Ei, ei, ei, mein gan- zes Geld ver- pufft! Ei!
Ambr.
ei, ei, ei, ei, ei, ei, ei, ei, ei, ei, ei, ei, ei, ei, ei, ei, ei, ei, ei! Ei!
Wirth
Ei, ei, ei, ei, ei, ei, ei, ei, ei! Ei!
Vc.
Cb.

No. 4. Romanze von dem verliebten Kater Mansor

Mansor hin den Pfad der Liebe schlich, den Pfad der Liebe schlich, der Kater Mansor.

Dialog*

Einzeln, recht nach seinem Herzen, stand das Häuschen da, das Zaïden, Za-

*Dialog: Gaston: "Was singt sie? Der Kater Mansor?" Ambrosio: "Bei Gott, vom Kater Mansor! Der macht Euch gewiß verliebte Streiche!"

*Dialog: [Inez:] "So hört die traurige Geschichte erst zu Ende!"

34
Ob. 1
Cl. 1
Vn. 1
Vn. 2
Va.
Inez
Vc.
Cb.
pp
Treu-e schwur, der fal- sche Man- sor, der har- te
37
poco rit.
Fl. 1
Ob. 1
Cl. 1
tr
ppp
pizz.
[pizz.]
a tempo
Man- - sor! Doch beim Mor- gen- strah- le

67

*Dies Ton hinunter ziehen.

No. 5. Seguidilla a dos

69

Sold, doch die bei uns im Sold. Und un- ser gan- zes

21
Ob. 1, 2
Cl. 1, 2
Vn. 1
Vn. 2
Va.
Gast.
Le- ben ist ih- nen hin- ge- ge- ben mit hei- ßer Lei- den-
pizz. arco pizz.
Vc.
pizz.
Cb.
25
a 2
vi-
-de
Fl. 1, 2
Ob. 1, 2
Cl. 1, 2
Springbogen
cresc.
[divisi]
Vn. 1
Vn. 2
Va.
Inez
Doch nie, daß es Euch Lei- den schafft!
Gast.
-schaft!
arco
Vc.
Cb.

72

Wenn's gilt, mit Män-nern strei- ten, wir schla-gen rasch da-

-rein, doch sind wir ge- gen Frau- en all-zeit gar zart und

fein, all- zeit gar zart und fein, all- zeit gar zart und fein.

42
C
Fl. 1, 2
Ob. 1, 2
Cl. 1, 2
Bn. 1, 2
Hn. 1, 2
Tpt. 1, 2
Timp.
Trgl.
Vn. 1
Vn. 2
Va.
Gast.
Vc.
Cb.
Springbogen
divisi
pizz.
D'rum lie-ben uns die Mäd- chen in je-dem Dorf und Städt- chen, wo wir uns las- sen

Fl. 1, 2
Ob. 1, 2
Cl. 1, 2
Vn. 1
Vn. 2
Va.
Inez
Gast.
Vc.
Cb.
a 2
divisi
arco
pizz.
Ja, wenn Sie schleu- nigst wie- der geh'n!
seh'n!
D
Etwas gemächlicher
Bn. 1, 2
Zwar le- ben wir in Freu- den bei Sang und Re- ben-

55
Ob. 1, 2
Bn. 1, 2
Vn. 1
Vn. 2
Va.
Gast.
Vc.
Cb.
pp
pizz.
p
-saft. _
Doch wirkt in
uns
die _
Weis-
heit
auch
59
Ob. 1, 2
Bn. 1, 2
Vn. 1
Vn. 2
Va.
Gast.
Vc.
Cb.
p
arco
pizz.
mit
be-
sond'-rer _
Kraft.
In
al-
ler _ Mu-
sen
Tem-
pel,
wir
nen-
nen uns E-

64
Ob. 1, 2
Bn. 1, 2
Vn. 1
Vn. 2
Va.
pizz.
p
Gast.
-xem- pel der höch- sten Wis- sen- schaft, in al- ler Mu- sen Tem- pel, wir
Vc.
69
Ob. 1, 2
p
Cl. 1, 2
p
Bn. 1, 2
p
Vn. 1
Vn. 2
Va.
Inez
Ei, wie ge- wis- sen-
Gast.
nen- nen uns E- xem- pel der höch- sten Wis- sen- schaft, der höch-sten Wis- sen-
Vc.

E
73
poco accel.
poco rit.
Frisch, wie am Anfang
a tempo
Fl. 1, 2
Ob. 1, 2
Cl. 1, 2
Bn. 1, 2
Hn. 1, 2
Vn. 1
arco
cresc.
Vn. 2
divisi
arco
[cresc.]
Va.
arco
Inez
-haft!
Gast.
-schaft!
D'rum le- ben die Stu- den-
Vc.
arco
Cb.
arco

Inez: Da's ein- mal denn muß sein!

Gast: -ten, es le- ben die Stu- den- ten! Es le- be, was sie

81
Fl. 1, 2
Ob. 1, 2
Cl. 1, 2
Bn. 1, 2
Hn. 1, 2
Hn. 3
Tpt. 1, 2
Trgl.
Vn. 1
Vn. 2
Va.
Inez
Gast.
Vc.
Cb.
1
p
pizz.
pizz.
pizz.
Das geb' ich auch noch d'rein, das geb' ich auch noch
lie- ben, es le- be, was sie lie- ben, es le- be, was sie lie- ben, es le- be, was sie

82

89
Ob. 1, 2
Vn. 1
pp
Vn. 2
Va.
Inez
Gast.
-ben, Dir ist mein Herz er- ge- ben; Dich o- der Kei- ne _ lieb' ich _
Vc.
Cb.
93
Ob. 1, 2
1
f
Hn. 1, 2
Vn. 1
Vn. 2
Va.
Inez
Mein Herr Stu- dent, ich dan- ke sehr, mein Herr Stu- dent, ich dan- ke _
Gast.
mehr, Dich o- der Kei- ne _ lieb' ich mehr, Dich o- der Kei- ne lieb' ich, lieb' ich
Vc.
Cb.
arco

Inez: sehr, ja ich dan- ke, dan- ke sehr!

Gast.: mehr, Dich o- der Kei- ne mehr!

No. 6. Terzett

Hn. 1, 2
Hn. 3, 4
Vn. 1
Vn. 2
Gast.
al- so frisch das Werk be- gon- nen
Vc. Cb.
p
Hn. 1, 2
Hn. 3, 4
Vn. 1
(sanft betont)
Vn. 2
(sanft betont)
Gast.
lie- ben-der In- struc- ti- on!
Pinto
f
Ja, es sei das Werk be-
Vc. Cb.

87

16
Hn. 1, 2
Hn. 3, 4
a 2
3
Vn. 1
Vn. 2
Gast.
-on,
lie- ben-der In- struc- ti- on!
Ambr.
Was da wird für Spaß er- son- nen, da- rauf freu- e ich mich schon!
Pinto
f
-on,
lie- ben-der In- struc- ti- on! Al- so frisch!
Vc.
Cb.
A
19
Ob. 1, 2
a 2
mf
p (sanft betont)
Cl. 1, 2
mf
p (sanft betont)
Bn. 1, 2
a 2
mf
p (sanft betont)
Hn. 1, 2
mf
Hn. 3, 4
4
p
Vn. 1
p
Vn. 2
p
Gast.
(zu Ambrosio)
Setz' Dich dort- hin sitt- sam,
Vc.
arco
f

89

28
Ob. 1, 2
Cl. 1, 2
Bn. 1, 2
Hn. 3, 4
3
Vn. 1
Vn. 2
pp
Va.
pp
Gast.
(zu Pinto)
G'ra- de recht nach mei- nem Sinn!
Nun komm'
Ambr.
rich- tig?
Pinto
O, für mich welch' ein Ge- winn!
Vc.
[arco]
pp
31
Vn. 1
pp
Vn. 2
divisi
Va.
divisi
Gast.
ich an Ih- rer Stel- le, tre- te ü- ber die- se Schwel-le flüch- tig,
Vc.

91

92

93

94

95

70
Ob. 1, 2
Cl. 1, 2
Bn. 1, 2
Hn. 1, 2
Hn. 3, 4
Vn. 1
Vn. 2
Va.
Gast.
Ambr.
Pinto
Vc.
Cb.
mf
f
p
cresc.
ff
arco
-treff- lich geh'n die Sa- chen! Ganz vor-
La-chen, hal- ten kann ich kaum das La- chen! Hal- ten kann ich kaum das
kann ich herr- lich ma- chen, gelt, das kann ich herr- lich ma- chen, herr- lich

73
Hn. 1, 2
Hn. 3, 4
Vn. 1
Vn. 2
Gast.
-treff- lich, ganz vor-treff- lich, ganz vor-treff-
Ambr.
La- chen, ganz vor-treff- lich, ganz vor-treff-
Pinto
ma- chen, ganz vor-treff- lich, ganz vor-treff-
76
D
Noch etwas lebhafter
Hn. 1, 2
Hn. 3, 4
Tpt. 1, 2
Vn. 1
Noch etwas lebhafter
Vn. 2
Gast.
-lich! Nun ge-
Ambr.
-lich!
Pinto
-lich!

98

Ambr.: Sie zer-tram-peln mir die Fü- ße!

Pinto: -lant! Wohl, ich stür- ze hin und küs- se!

Gast.: Sit- zen blei- ben, Fräu-lein Braut! Noch ein- mal!

Pinto: Nun auf- ge-

100

101
Meno mosso
Fl. 1, 2
Ob. 1, 2
Meno mosso
Vn. 1
Vn. 2
Va.
Gast.
O, ich
Ambr.
(falsett)
Wel- che Kühn- heit!
Vc.
Cb.
105
Ob. 1, 2
solo
Vn. 1
Vn. 2
Va.
Gast.
kann _ die- sem Reiz nicht wi- der- ste- hen, hier zu Ih- ren Fü- ßen
Ambr.
Vc.
Cb.

102

*N.B. Sollte dem Sänger Ambrosio keine genug ausgiebige Fistel zu Gebote stehen, so empfiehlt sich angegebener Strich von ⊕ zum ⊕ . In diesem Falle hat Pinto die unten klein gedruckten Noten [mm. 115–118/141] zu singen.
Scenische Bemerkung für den Fall des Sprungs: Gaston giebt Pinto ein Zeichen, zugleich mit ihm niederzuknien, was dieser sofort befolgt.

120
Ob. 1, 2
1
p
Vn. 1
p
pp
Vn. 2
p
pp
Va.
p
Gast.
-zeih- ung ich ge- wann!
Ambr.
Gott, man ist ja
divisi
Vc.
Cb.
123
Ob. 1, 2
a 2
Vn. 1
solo
Vn. 2
p
Va.
p
ossia
nicht, ja
Ambr.
nicht, ja
Vc.

126
G
Fl. 1, 2
a 2
f
Ob. 1, 2
f
Bn. 1, 2
[a 2]
f
Hn. 1, 2
f
Hn. 3, 4
a 2
f
Tpt. 1, 2
f
Timp.
f
Vn. 1
[tutti]
f
Vn. 2
f
Va.
Ambr.
nicht von Eis, man ist ja nicht von Eis!
Pinto
Schön, vor-treff-lich, will's pro- bi- ren, will's pro- bi-ren, will's pro- bi-
Vc. Cb.
pizz.
[arco]
mf
f

130
Fl. 1, 2
a 2
f
Ob. 1, 2
f
1
Cl. 1, 2
a 2
f
Bn. 1, 2
Hn. 1, 2
Hn. 3, 4
a 2
Tpt. 1, 2
Timp.
in B-F♯
Vn. 1
p
Vn. 2
p
Va.
solo
f
Ambr.
Wel- che Kühn- heit!
Pinto
(macht es noch)
-ren!
Sap- per-
Vc.
Cb.
pizz.
p

107

108

143
H
Ein wenig zurückhaltend
Fl. 1, 2
Ob. 1, 2
Cl. 1, 2
Bn. 1, 2
Ein wenig zurückhaltend
Vn. 1
Vn. 2
Va.
p
p
Gast.
d'ran! Jet- zo wei- ter: "Hol- de
(Pinto steht auf)
Pinto
(hervortretend)
Vc.
f
p
Cb.
p
146
Ob. 1, 2
1
p espress.
Vn. 1
pp
Vn. 2
Va.
Gast.
Schö- ne, bin ich von dem Glück er-
Vc.
pizz.
pp
Cb.
pizz.

110

158
Vorwärts!
Fl. 1, 2
Ob. 1, 2
Bn. 1, 2
Vorwärts!
Vn. 1
Vn. 2
Va.
Gast.
Nur ver- sucht, es wird schon geh'n, es wird schon
Pinto
lern' ich schwer-lich!
Vc.
Cb.
161
J
molto string.
Fl. 1, 2
Ob. 1, 2
Cl. 1, 2
Bn. 1, 2
divisi
molto string.
Vn. 1
Vn. 2
Va.
Gast.
geh'n!
Pinto
Hol- de Schö- ne,
arco
Vc.
Cb.
pesante

164
[1]
Fl. 1, 2
Ob. 1, 2
Cl. 1, 2
Bn. 1, 2
Vn. 1
Vn. 2
Va.
Pinto
die sehr schön, ich bin toll ganz vor Ent-
Vc.
Cb.
167
a 2
-zü-cken, daß Sie zu- cker- sü- ßes We- sen mich zu Ih- ren Mann er-
cresc.
cresc.

170
poco rit.
K
Fl. 1, 2
Ob. 1, 2
Cl. 1, 2
Vn. 1
Vn. 2
Va.
Gast.
Pinto
Vc.
Cb.
(tr)
mf
p
pp
[1]
1
pizz.
Bli- cken Sie in's Aug' ihr
-le- sen und mich krö- nen,—
174
molto rit.
Bn. 1, 2
Hn. 1, 2
espress.
solo
(macht es Pinto vor)
glü- hend heiß:

114

115

192
Fl. 1, 2
Ob. 1, 2
Cl. 1, 2
Bn. 1, 2
Vn. 1
Vn. 2
Va.
Gast.
Ambr.
Vc.
Cb.
p
mf
cresc.
rasch die sü- ße Spei- se von den Lip- pen sich ge- nascht, die al- lein der Lie- be
ach, wie wird mir doch so
195
a 2
f
ff
tr
ei- gen!
warm, mir wird so warm!
senza sord.

198
Fl. 1, 2
Ob. 1, 2
Cl. 1, 2
Vn. 1
Vn. 2
Va.
Gast.
Ambr.
Pinto
Vc.
Cb.
senza sord.
senza sord.
senza sord.
Frei- lich, frei- lich!
(mit natürlicher Stimme)
(zu Gaston)
(tr)
Soll ich dann be-reit mich zei-gen?
(Ambrosio in Pintos Arme sinkend)
Frisch d'rauf los, frisch d'rauf
202
Ob. 1, 2
[a 2]
rit.
Vn. 1
rit.
Vn. 2
Va.
Gast.
Ambr.
(falsett)
Ach, der Lie- - be Macht ist
Pinto
(giebt Ambrosio einen tüchtigen Kuß)
los!
Vc.
Cb.

118

119

Gast: -stehen, wie nach aller-neustem Schnitt zu der Braut der Bräut'gam
Ambr: gehen, wenn er vor die Braut so tritt, nimmt er ihr die Füße
Pinto: -stehen, wie nach aller-neustem Schnitt vor die Braut der Bräut'gam

Gast: tritt. Bravo, bravo, so wird's geh'n, herrlich werden Sie's ver-
Ambr: mit. Bravo, brav', ich muß gesteh'n, besser kann es gar nicht
Pinto: tritt. Bravo, bravo, so wird's geh'n, Kinder-leicht ist's zu ver-

218
Bn. 1, 2
Vn. 1
Vn. 2
Va.
Gast.
Ambr.
Pinto
Vc.
Cb.
f
sul G
-steh'n, wie nach al- ler- neu- stem Schnitt zu der Braut der Bräut'- gam
geh'n, wenn er vor die Braut so tritt, nimmt er ihr die Fü- ße
-steh'n, bra- vo, bra- vo, so wird's ge- hen, Kin-der-leicht ist's zu ver- steh'n, wie nach al- ler- neu- stem
222
N
pp
tr
tritt, zu der Braut der Bräut'-gam tritt! Bra- vo, bra- vo, so wird's geh'n!
mit, nimmt er ihr die Fü- ße mit, nimmt er ihr die Fü- ße mit!
Schnitt zu der Braut der Bräut'-gam tritt! Bra- vo, bra- vo, so wird's geh'n!

226
Vn. 1
Vn. 2
Va.
Gast.
Pinto
Vc.
Cb.
p
pp
(zu Gaston)
Schö- nen Dank!
Gar nicht nö- thig!
230
O
Cl. 1, 2
Bn. 1, 2
Vn. 1
Vn. 2
Va.
Ambr.
Pinto
Vc.
Cb.
pizz.
(zu Ambrosio)
Gro- ße Schuld!
Gern' er- bö- tig!

234
Vn. 1
Vn. 2
Va.
Gast.
Pinto
Vc.
Cb.
p
(zu Gaston)
So die Bli- cke?
Zum Er- ge- ben!
arco
238
rit.
-de
a tempo
a 2
mf
Ob. 1, 2
Cl. 1, 2
Bn. 1, 2
Hn. 1, 2
Vn. 1
Vn. 2
Va.
Gast.
Ambr.
Pinto
Vc.
Cb.
f
Bra- vo,
(falsett)
O mein Le- ben! Bra- vo,
(zu Ambrosio)
Sü- ße Schö- ne!
Bra- vo,
pizz.
arco

242
stringendo al Fine
a 2
Fl. 1, 2
Ob. 1, 2
Cl. 1, 2
Bn. 1, 2
Hn. 1, 2
Hn. 3, 4
pizz.
stringendo al Fine
Vn. 1
Vn. 2
Va.
Gast.
bra- vo, _ so _ wird's ge- hen, herr- lich wer- den _ Sie's ver- ste- hen, wie nach
Ambr.
brav', ich muß ge- ste- hen, bes- ser kann es _ gar _ nicht ge- hen, wenn er
Pinto
bra- vo, so wird's ge- hen, Kin- der- leicht ist's zu ver- ste- hen, wie nach
Vc.
Cb.

246
Ob. 1, 2
Cl. 1, 2
Bn. 1, 2
Hn. 1, 2
Hn. 3, 4
Vn. 1
tr
p
Gast.
al- ler- neu- stem Schnitt vor die Braut der _ Bräut'- gam tritt. Herr-lich
Ambr.
vor _ die _ Braut so tritt, nimmt er ihr _ die _ Fü- ße mit. Bes- ser
Pinto
al- ler- neu- stem Schnitt vor die Braut der _ Bräut'- gam tritt. Kin- der-
250
Ob. 1, 2
a 2
cresc.
Cl. 1, 2
a 2
cresc.
Bn. 1, 2
a 2
cresc.
Hn. 1, 2
cresc.
Hn. 3, 4
cresc.
Tpt. 1, 2
pp
cresc.
Vn. 1
(tr)
Gast.
wer- den Sie's ver- steh'n, ___ bra- vo, bra- vo, so wird's geh'n, _______ ganz _ vor-
Ambr.
kann es gar nicht geh'n, ___ bra- vo, brav', ich muß ge- steh'n, _______ ganz _ vor-
Pinto
-leicht ist's zu ver- steh'n, ___ bra- vo, bra- vo, so wird's geh'n, _______ ganz _ vor-

254
Fl. 1, 2
Ob. 1, 2
Cl. 1, 2
Bn. 1, 2
Hn. 1, 2
Hn. 3, 4
Tpt. 1, 2
a 2
Timp.
Vn. 1
(tr)
Vn. 2
Va.
divisi
Gast.
-treff- lich, wun- der- schön, herr- lich, herr- lich, herr- lich, herr- lich wird das
Ambr.
-treff- lich, wun- der- schön, herr- lich, herr- lich, herr- lich, herr- lich wird das
Pinto
-treff- lich, wun- der- schön, herr- lich, herr- lich, herr- lich, herr- lich wird das
Vc.
pizz.
Cb.
pizz.

257
P
Più mosso
Fl. 1, 2
a 2
tr
f
Ob. 1, 2
a 2
tr
f
Cl. 1, 2
a 2
tr
f
Bn. 1, 2
[a 2]
mf
Hn. 1, 2
mf
Hn. 3, 4
mf
Tpt. 1, 2
Timp.
Più mosso
Vn. 1
fff
p
Vn. 2
fff
p
Va.
fff
p
Gast.
geh'n, herr- lich, herr- lich wird das_ geh'n! Herr- lich,
Ambr.
geh'n, herr- lich, herr- lich wird das_ geh'n! Herr- lich,
Pinto
geh'n, herr- lich, herr- lich wird das geh'n! Herr- lich,
Vc.
arco
ff
p
Cb.
arco
ff
p

260
Fl. 1, 2
Ob. 1, 2
Cl. 1, 2
Bn. 1, 2
tr
Hn. 1, 2
Hn. 3, 4
Vn. 1
Vn. 2
Va.
Gast.
herr- lich wird das geh'n, ganz herr- lich wird das
Ambr.
herr- lich wird das geh'n, ganz herr- lich wird das
Pinto
herr- lich wird das geh'n, ganz herr- lich wird das
Vc.
tr
Cb.
tr

263
Fl. 1, 2
mf
Ob. 1, 2
mf
Cl. 1, 2
mf
Bn. 1, 2
[a 2]
mf
tr
Hn. 1, 2
Hn. 3, 4
Vn. 1
Vn. 2
Va.
Gast.
geh'n, herr- lich, herr- lich wird das geh'n, ganz
Ambr.
geh'n, herr- lich, herr- lich wird das geh'n, ganz
Pinto
geh'n, herr- lich, herr- lich wird das geh'n, ganz
Vc.
tr
f
p
Cb.
tr
f
p

129

269
Fl. 1, 2
Ob. 1, 2
Cl. 1, 2
a 2
Bn. 1, 2
Hn. 1, 2
Hn. 3, 4
Tpt. 1, 2
Tpt. 3
tr
tr
Timp.
Vn. 1
mf
p
cresc.
Vn. 2
mf
p
cresc.
Va.
p
Gast.
herr- lich, so wird's ge- hen,
Ambr.
La- chen, kaum das La- chen,
Pinto
herr- lich, so wird's ge- hen, ganz vor- treff- lich, ganz vor-
Vc.
p

131

275
Sehr schnell
Fl. 1, 2
Ob. 1, 2
Cl. 1, 2
Bn. 1, 2
cresc.
ff
Hn. 1, 2
Hn. 3, 4
Tpt. 1, 2
Tpt. 3
Timp.
Sehr schnell
Vn. 1
Vn. 2
Va.
Gast.
-hen, herr- lich, herr- lich wird es geh'n, herr- lich, herr- lich wird es geh'n!
Ambr.
-chen. Herr- lich, herr- lich wird es geh'n, herr- lich, herr- lich wird es geh'n!
Pinto
-hen, herr- lich, herr- lich wird es geh'n, herr- lich, herr- lich wird es geh'n!
Vc.
Cb.

278
Fl. 1, 2
Ob. 1, 2
Cl. 1, 2
Bn. 1, 2
Hn. 1, 2
Hn. 3, 4
Tpt. 1, 2
Tpt. 3
Timp.
Vn. 1
Vn. 2
Va.
Vc.
Cb.
fff
ff
tr

No. 7. Finale

4
Fl. 1, 2
Ob. 1, 2
[1]
mf
Cl. 1, 2
Bn. 1, 2
p
Hn. 1, 2
p
Hn. 3, 4
p
Tpt. 1, 2
p
Trb. 1, 2
Trb. 3
Tb.
Timp.
B. Drum
divisi
Vn. 1
p
p
Vn. 2
p
divisi
Va.
p
(Inez stößt mit Gaston an)
Inez
Auf das Wohl- er- geh'n der Gä- ste!
Gast.
Schön be-
Pinto
Vc.
p
Cb.
p

136

Inez: Gut wird, was man ger- ne thut!

Gast.: -wir- thest uns auf's Be- ste! Auf das

Inez: Schön bedankt!

Gast.: Wohl der schönen Inez!

(stößt mit Inez an, wendet sich dann zu Pinto)

20
Fl. 1, 2
Cl. 1, 2
Bn. 1, 2
[a 2]
Hn. 1, 2
Hn. 3, 4
Trb. 1, 2
a 2
Trb. 3
Tb.
[in D-B]
Timp.
B. Drum
Vn. 1
Vn. 2
pizz.
arco
Va.
[pizz.]
arco
Inez
Gast.
(zu Inez)
Wel-che ö- de Men- schen-
Pinto
(weist ihn kauend ab)
Ist schon gut, ist schon gut, ist schon gut!
Vc.
pizz.
Cb.
pizz.

24
Fl. 1, 2
Cl. 1, 2
Bn. 1, 2
Vn. 1
Vn. 2
Va.
Inez
(zu Gaston)
Die kommt nicht so leicht in Glut!
Gast.
-see- le!
Vc.
arco
Cb.
arco
27
Fl. 1, 2
Cl. 1, 2
Bn. 1, 2
Vn. 1
Vn. 2
Va.
Gast.
Vc.
Cb.

31
B
Tempo moderato
Fl. 1, 2
Cl. 1, 2
Bn. 1, 2
Tempo moderato
Vn. 1
p grazioso
Vn. 2
Va.
Gast.
f (beiseite)
Nein, das werd' ich nim-mer lei- den, daß ein sol- ches Kalbs- ge- sicht zum Al-
Vc.
pizz.
mf
Cb.
pizz.
mf
35
Fl. 1, 2
Cl. 1, 2
Bn. 1, 2
Vn. 1
pp
Vn. 2
Va.
Gast.
-ta- re sollt' ge- lei- ten ei- nen En- gel hold und
Vc.

142

143

D
51
Fl. 1, 2
Ob. 1, 2
Cl. 1, 2
Bn. 1, 2
Vn. 1
Vn. 2
Va.
pizz.
Inez
Gott be- wahr' vor sol- chem Frei- er mich mein gan- zes Le- ben
Gast.
Ambr.
Solch' ein Töl- pel zieht auf Frei- te nach der schön- sten Don- na
Pinto
ja!
Vc.
Cb.

54
Fl. 1, 2
Ob. 1, 2
Cl. 1, 2
Bn. 1, 2
Vn. 1
Vn. 2
Va.
Inez
p
lang! Am Al- tar zur Hoch- zeits- fei- er! Ach, da wird mir
Gast.
Ambr.
aus, geb' der Teu- fel ihm's Ge- lei- te! Hof- fent-lich wird
Pinto
Vc.
Cb.

58
Fl. 1, 2
Ob. 1, 2
Cl. 1, 2
Bn. 1, 2
Hn. 1, 2
Hn. 3, 4
Vn. 1
Vn. 2
Va.
Inez
angst und bang, ach, da wird mir angst und bang, ja, ja, ja, ja, da
Gast.
Nein, das werd' ich nim- mer
Ambr.
nichts da- raus, hof- fent-lich wird nichts da- raus! Ha, solch' ein Töl- pel zieht auf
Pinto
Gu- ter
Vc.
Cb.

147

E
66
Fl. 1, 2
Ob. 1, 2
Cl. 1, 2
Bn. 1, 2
Hn. 1, 2
Hn. 3, 4
a 2
Tpt. 1, 2
in E♭-B♭
Timp.
divisi
(Doppelgriff)
Vn. 1
Vn. 2
Va.
Inez
Gast.
Da-rum als ein ech- ter Rit- ter rett' ich die be-dräng- te
Ambr.
Pinto
Vc.
Cb.

Pinto: Dieses Hähnchen schmeckt nicht bitter und das Weinchen thut kein

74
Fl. 1, 2
Ob. 1, 2
Cl. 1, 2
Bn. 1, 2
Vn. 1
divisi
Vn. 2
arco
Va.
arco
Inez
Lie-ber hin-ter'm Klos- ter- git-ter, als solch' ei-nen Mann ge- freit, lie-ber
Gast.
Da- rum als ein ech-ter Rit-ter rett' ich die be- droh- te
Ambr.
Solch' ein Töl- pel, solch' ein Töl- pel auf
Pinto
Leid, die-ses Hähn- chen schmeckt nicht bit- ter und das Wein- chen thut kein
Vc.
Cb.

78
Vorwärts!
Fl. 1, 2
Ob. 1, 2
Cl. 1, 2
Bn. 1, 2
Hn. 1, 2
Hn. 3, 4
Tpt. 1, 2
a 2
Vorwärts!
Vn. 1
Vn. 2
Va.
Inez
hin-ter'm Klos- ter-git- ter, als solch' ei-nen Mann ge- freit!
Gast.
(tritt an die Tafel, höchst heiter)
Maid, die be-droh- te Maid! Schenkt
Ambr.
Freit', geb' der Teu- fel ihm's Ge- leit'!
Pinto
Leid, und das Wein- chen thut kein Leid!
Vc.
Cb.

82
Fl. 1, 2
Ob. 1, 2
Cl. 1, 2
Bn. 1, 2
Hn. 1, 2
Hn. 3, 4
Tpt. 1, 2
Vn. 1
Vn. 2
Va.
Gast.
2
fp
a 2
fp
p
pizz.
f
pizz.
f
ein, schenkt ein! Heut' soll der Wein in vol- len

86
Fl. 1, 2
Ob. 1, 2
Cl. 1, 2
Tpt. 1, 2
Vn. 1
Vn. 2
Va.
Gast.
Vc.
p
p
1
p
p
[arco]
p
[arco]
p
p
Strö- men flie- ßen, sollt' Al- le mit- ge- nie- ßen! Al- le her-

-bei, trin- ket nun frei; heut' soll der Wein in vol- len Strö- men

96
F
Fl. 1, 2
Ob. 1, 2
Cl. 1, 2
Bn. 1, 2
a 2
mf
Hn. 1, 2
a 2
mf
Hn. 3, 4
a 2
mf
Tpt. 1, 2
a 2
mf
Vn. 1
p
Vn. 2
p
Va.
Inez
f
Was fällt Ih- nen ein! Was
Gast.
flie- ßen!
Ambr.
f
Er muß ein Narr wohl sein, hat
Pinto
f
Ei! Ei! Er muß ein Narr wohl
Vc.

155

106
Immer vorwärts
Fl. 1, 2
Ob. 1, 2
Cl. 1, 2
Bn. 1, 2
a 2
Hn. 1, 2
Hn. 3, 4
Trb. 1, 2
Trb. 3
Tb.
Immer vorwärts
Vn. 1
Vn. 2
Va.
S
Wein, es le- be der Wein, es le- be der Wein, es
A
Wein, es le- be der Wein, es le- be der Wein, es
T
Wein, es le- be der Wein, es le- be der Wein, es
B
Wein, es le- be der Wein, es le- be der Wein, es
Vc.
[arco]
Cb.

111
Fl. 1, 2
Ob. 1, 2
Cl. 1, 2
Bn. 1, 2
Hn. 1, 2
Hn. 3, 4
Trb. 1, 2
Trb. 3
Tb.
Vn. 1
Vn. 2
Va.
S
A
T
B
Vc.
Cb.
a 2
f
ff
le- be der Wein, es le- be, es le- be der Wein!

158

159

160

161

mehr noch könn- te mir scha- den; es ist mir,

163

152
a 2
Fl. 1, 2
Ob. 1, 2
Cl. 1, 2
Bn. 1, 2
Hn. 1, 2
Hn. 3, 4
Tpt. 1, 2
tr
in F-C
Timp.
Vn. 1
Vn. 2
Va.
Gast.
Schön-heit!
Es le- be die Lie- be!
S
Die Schön- heit! Die
A
Die Schön- heit! Die
T
Die Schön- heit! Die
B
Die Schön- heit! Die
Vc.
Cb.

157
Fl. 1, 2
Ob. 1, 2
Cl. 1, 2
Bn. 1, 2
Hn. 1, 2
Hn. 3, 4
Tpt. 1, 2
Tpt. 3
Timp.
tr
in C-G
mf
Vn. 1
Vn. 2
(zu den Herren)
Inez
Es le- be die Weis- heit! Die
S
Lie- be! Die Weis- heit!
A
Lie- be! Die Weis- heit!
T
Lie- be! Die Weis- heit!
B
Lie- be! Die Weis- heit!
Vc. Cb.

166

167

172
Fl. 1, 2
Ob. 1, 2
Bn. 1, 2
ff
Tpt. 1, 2
a 2
fp
Tpt. 3
Trb. 1, 2
Trb. 3
Tb.
Timp.
Vn. 1
Vn. 2
S
le- be die Lie- be, die Weis- heit, die Stär- ke, es
A
le- be die Lie- be, die Weis- heit, die Stär- ke, es
T
le- be die Lie- be, die Weis- heit, die Stär- ke, es
B
le- be die Lie- be, die Weis- heit, die Stär- ke, es
Vc.
Cb.

169

Wein, es lebe der Wein, es lebe die Schönheit, die

Lie- be, es le- be die Weis- heit, die

192
Fl. 1, 2
Ob. 1, 2
Cl. 1, 2
Bn. 1, 2
Hn. 1, 2
Hn. 3, 4
Timp.
Vn. 1
Vn. 2
S
Stär- ke, es le- be die Weis- heit, die Stär- -
A
Stär- ke, es le- be die Weis- heit, die Stär- -
T
Stär- ke, es le- be die Weis- heit, die Stär- -
B
Stär- ke, es le- be die Weis- heit, die Stär- -
Vc.
Cb.

197
G.P.
Fl. 1, 2
Ob. 1, 2
Cl. 1, 2
Bn. 1, 2
Hn. 1, 2
Hn. 3, 4
Tpt. 1, 2
Tpt. 3
Trb. 1, 2
Trb. 3
Tb.
Timp.
G.P.
Vn. 1
Vn. 2
(Pinto will anstoßen und taumelt)
(lange halten)
Pinto
Sie le- Es
(Sie stoßen an)
S
-ke, sie le- be!
A
-ke, sie le- be!
T
-ke, sie le- be!
B
-ke, sie le- be!
Vc.
Cb.

202
rit.
Fl. 1, 2
Ob. 1, 2
[1]
pp
Cl. 1, 2
in A
a 2
Bn. 1, 2
Hn. 1, 2
Hn. 3, 4
Timp.
[B♭ to A]
B. Drum
Vn. 1
pizz.
p
Vn. 2
divisi
Va.
Inez
Gast.
Don Pin- to, die Reih' ist an Ih- nen!
Ambr.
(beiseite, parodirend)
Ist schon gut, ist schon gut, ist schon gut, ist schon
Pinto
(lallend)
ist mir,— ich mer-ke,— Ich kann Euch da- mit nicht
Vc.
Cb.

175

212
rit.
a tempo
a 2
tr
ff
in B♭
Fl. 1, 2
Ob. 1, 2
Cl. 1, 2
Bn. 1, 2
Hn. 1, 2
Hn. 3, 4
Timp.
B. Drum
Trgl.
ppp
pizz.
Vn. 1
Vn. 2
Va.
Pinto
Nun, es le- be, es le- be der Ma- gen!
S
A
T
B
fff
Ha, ha, ha, ha, ha, ha, ha,
Vc.
Cb.

177

222
J
Etwas gemächlicher
Fl. 1, 2
Ob. 1, 2
Cl. 1, 2
a 2
Bn. 1, 2
Hn. 1, 2
Timp.
(tr)
Etwas gemächlicher
Vn. 1
Vn. 2
divisi
pizz.
Va.
divisi
pizz.
Gast.
Der Ge- ber so herr- li- cher
S
gen!
A
gen!
T
gen!
B
gen!
hervortretend
Vc.
Cb.

227
Fl. 1, 2
Ob. 1, 2
Cl. 1, 2
Vn. 1
Vn. 2
Va.
Gast.
Freu- den zieht stets sich zu- rück so be- schei- den!
Vc.
Cb.
232
Tpt. 1, 2
a 2
pp
Vn. 1
p
divisi
mf
f
Vn. 2
f
Va.
f
Gast.
Heut' sei ihm ein Vi- vat ge- bracht, ihm sei heut' ein
Ambr.
Heut' sei ihm ein Vi- vat ge- bracht, ihm sei heut' ein
pizz.
Vc.
f
Cb.
f

238
rit.
B. Drum
pp
Vn. 1
pizz.
arco
ff
Vn. 2
pizz.
pp
Va.
Gast.
Vi- vat ge- bracht!
Ambr.
Vi- vat ge- bracht!
(mit zitternder Stimme)
Pinto
Ein Vi- - vat, ja, ja, gu- te
Vc.
ff
Cb.
244
a tempo
Fl. 1, 2
f
Ob. 1, 2
Cl. 1, 2
Bn. 1, 2
(Pinto rüttelnd)
Fein mun- ter und lu- stig ge- blie- ben!
(zu Pinto)
Gu- te Nacht, gu- te
(will einschlafen)
Nacht! Ja, mun-ter,—

181

hold und treu ge- blie- ben, was wir lie- ben, was wir lie- ben, was uns hold und treu ge- blie- ben, was wir

Was wir

Inez: lie- ben, lie- ben, hold und

S: lie- ben, was wir lie- ben, was uns hold und treu ge-

A: lie- ben, was wir lie- ben, was uns hold und treu ge-

T: lie- ben, was wir lie- ben, was uns hold und treu ge-

B: lie- ben, was wir lie- ben, was uns hold und treu ge-

258
Fl. 1, 2
Ob. 1, 2
Cl. 1, 2
Bn. 1, 2
Hn. 1, 2
Vn. 1
Vn. 2
Va.
Inez
treu, hold und treu.
S
-blie- ben, was wir lie- ben! Der da schickt sich nicht zum Lie- ben, der da schickt sich nicht zum
A
-blie- ben, was wir lie- ben! Der da schickt sich nicht zum Lie- ben, der da schickt sich nicht zum
T
-blie- ben, was wir lie- ben! Der da schickt sich nicht zum Lie- ben, der da schickt sich nicht zum
B
-blie- ben, was wir lie- ben! Der da schickt sich nicht zum Lie- ben, der da schickt sich nicht zum
Vc.

(Gaston hat sich unterdessen an Pinto gemacht und ihm den Brief aus dem Wams gezogen)

Inez: Der ____ da __ schickt sich nicht zum Lie- ben, der da

S: Lie- ben, nein, nein, nein, nein, der da schickt sich nicht zum Lie- ben, nicht zum Lie- ben, nein, nein, nein, nein, der da

A: Lie- ben, nein, nein, nein, nein, der da schickt sich nicht zum Lie- ben, nicht zum Lie- ben, nein, nein, nein, nein, der da

T: Lie- ben, nein, nein, nein, nein, der da schickt sich nicht zum Lie- ben, nicht zum Lie- ben, nein, nein, nein, nein, der da

B: Lie- ben, nein, nein, nein, nein, der da schickt sich nicht zum Lie- ben, nicht zum Lie- ben, nein, nein, nein, nein, der da

264
K
1
Fl. 1, 2
Ob. 1, 2
Cl. 1, 2
Bn. 1, 2
Hn. 1, 2
Trgl.
Vn. 1
pizz.
f
Vn. 2
pizz.
f
Va.
pizz.
f
Inez
schickt sich nicht zum Lie- ben!
Gast.
(hervortretend)
Die- sen Brief hier sich zu rau- ben, ist kein
S
f
pp
(Der Chor immer mit größter Discretion)
schickt sich nicht zum Lie- ben! Was wir lie- ben, was wir lie- ben, was uns hold und treu ge- blie- ben, was wir
A
schickt sich nicht zum Lie- ben! Was wir lie- ben, was wir lie- ben, was uns hold und treu ge- blie- ben, was wir
T
schickt sich nicht zum Lie- ben! Was wir lie- ben, was wir lie- ben, was uns hold und treu ge- blie- ben, was wir
B
schickt sich nicht zum Lie- ben! Was wir lie- ben, was wir lie- ben, was uns hold und treu ge- blie- ben, was wir
Vc.
arco
[pizz.]
f
Cb.
[pizz.]
f

Gast.: Dieb- stahl, sollt' ich glau- ben, denn was auch Pa- pa ge-

S: lie- ben, was wir lie- ben, was uns hold und treu ge- blie- ben, was wir lie- ben, was wir

A: lie- ben, was wir lie- ben, was uns hold und treu ge- blie- ben, was wir lie- ben, was wir

T: lie- ben, was wir lie- ben, was uns hold und treu ge- blie- ben, was wir lie- ben, was wir

B: lie- ben, was wir lie- ben, was uns hold und treu ge- blie- ben, was wir lie- ben, was wir

188

189

L
Sehr gemächlich
279
Fl. 1, 2
Ob. 1, 2
Cl. 1, 2
Bn. 1, 2
Hn. 1, 2
Hn. 3, 4
pp
2
Sehr gemächlich
arco
Vn. 1
Vn. 2
Va.
p
Gast.
(zum Chor gewendet)
-zu! Seht, da ist er ein- ge- schla- fen, tragt ihn in des Bet- tes
S
A
T
B
-ben!
Vc.
Cb.
[arco]

*Bei dieser Stelle sollen die Streicher so abwechseln, daß, während ein Theil die Sordinen auf- und absetzt, der andere Theil weiterspielt.

193

M rit.

Gast: lacht! Laßt ihn schla- fen, laßt ihn

S: Ei, der mag be- trun-ken sein!

A: Steif und fest schlief er hier ein! Mun-ter, mun-ter, mun-ter! *(wollen ihn aufmerken)*

T: Ei, der mag be- trun-ken sein! Mun-ter, mun-ter, mun-ter! *(wollen ihn aufmerken)*

B: Steif und fest schlief er hier ein!

291
molto rit.
a tempo
pp
p
a 2
Ob. 1, 2
Cl. 1, 2
Bn. 1, 2
Vn. 1
Vn. 2
Va.
Gast.
Vc.
Cb.
(beiseite)
schla- fen! Sei- nen Brief hab' ich ge- bor- gen, noch zur Stun- de reis' ich
295
solo
(zum Chor)
fort. __ In die Kam- mer tragt ihn dort, in die Kam- mer tragt ihn

Bis zum Schluß im leichtesten *pp*
Sehr gemächlich ♩. **wie früher** ♩.

N
311
Fl. 1, 2
Ob. 1, 2
Cl. 1, 2
Bn. 1, 2
Hn. 1, 2
Hn. 3, 4
[tutti]
pizz.
con sord.
arco
Vn. 1
Vn. 2
Va.
Gast.
sacht!
Lei- se, lei- se, lei- se, sacht!
S
dort ___ soll er __ zur Ru- he geh'n!
Mor- gen mag er sel- ber
A
dort ___ soll er __ zur Ru- he geh'n!
Mor- gen mag _ er ___ sel- ber __
T
dort soll er __ zur Ru- he geh'n!
Mor- gen mag er sel- ber
B
dort soll er __ zur Ru- he geh'n!
Mor- gen mag er sel- ber
Vc.
Cb.

318
Fl. 1, 2
[a 2]
pp
Ob. 1, 2
pp
Cl. 1, 2
Bn. 1, 2
pp
Hn. 1, 2
pp
Hn. 3, 4
Vn. 1
Vn. 2
Va.
pizz.
Gast.
S
seh'n, ob er wei- ter rei- sen will. Da- rum lei-
A
seh'n, ob er wei- ter rei- sen will. Da- rum lei- se, lei- se, sacht, daß der Schlä- fer
T
seh'n, ob er wei- ter rei- sen will. Lei- se, sacht,
B
seh'n, ob er wei- ter rei- sen will. Lei- se, lei-
Vc.
pizz.
ppp
Cb.
[con sord.]
pizz.
ppp

324
[a 2]
Picc. 1, 2
Fl. 1, 2
(Picc. 1, 2)
Ob. 1, 2
Cl. 1, 2
Bn. 1, 2
Hn. 1, 2
Hn. 3, 4
Trgl.
Vn. 1
Vn. 2
Va.
Gast.
S
A
T
B
Vc.
Cb.
pp
ppp
[1]
pizz.
senza sord.
-se, da- rum lei- se, da- rum lei- se, stil- le, still, still,
nicht er-wacht, da-rum lei- se, lei- se, sacht, daß der Schlä-fer nicht er-wacht, still, still,
lei- se, sacht, tragt leis' und sacht, tragt leis' und sacht, still, still,
-se, lei- se, lei- se, still, still,

199

338
Vn. 1
Vn. 2
Va.
Gast.
S
A
T
B
Vc.
Cb.
con sord.
[arco]
pp sempre
arco
pp
leis' und sacht, daß der Schlä- fer nicht er- wacht! Dort soll er zur Ru- he geh'n,
ihn lei- se, da- rum
344
P
gestopft
Tpt. 1, 2
fp
wis- sen nicht, wie ihm ge- scheh'n. Ru- hig,
lei- se, lei- se, sacht, da- rum lei- se, lei- se, sacht, lei- se,
lei- se, sacht, lei- se, sacht, ru- hig,

201

358
Fl. 1, 2
Ob. 1, 2
Cl. 1, 2
Hn. 1, 2
Vn. 1
Vn. 2
Va.
Gast.
S
A
T
B
Vc.
Cb.
pizz.
pp
p
mf
- hig, lei- - - se, lei- se, stil- le, still! Ru-
- hig, lei- - - se, lei- se, stil- le, still!
- hig, lei- - - se, lei- se, stil- le, still,

365
Ob. 1, 2
Cl. 1, 2
Bn. 1, 2
Hn. 1, 2
1
pp
Vn. 1
arco
espress.
Vn. 2
Va.
Gast.
Tragt ihn leis' und sacht, daß er nicht er- wacht,
S
-hig, seid ru- hig, lei- se, still,
A
-hig, seid ru- hig, lei- se, still,
T
-hig, seid ru- hig, lei- se, still,
B
still, da- rum tragt ihn leis' und sacht, daß der Schlä- fer nicht er-wacht, still,
Vc.
Cb.

Q
372
Cl. 1, 2
Bn. 1, 2
Vn. 1
Gast.
daß er nicht er- wacht, daß der Schlä- fer
Vc.
Cb.
378
Cl. 1, 2
Bn. 1, 2
Hn. 1, 2
1 gestopft
B. Drum
Vn. 1
Gast.
nicht er- wacht!
(Sie tragen Pinto vorsichtig durch die Thür' in's Innere des Hauses)
S
still, still, still, still!
A
still, still, still, still!
T
still, still, still, still!
B
still, still, still, still!
[arco]
Vc.
Cb.

Ende des ersten Aufzuges

Entr'act

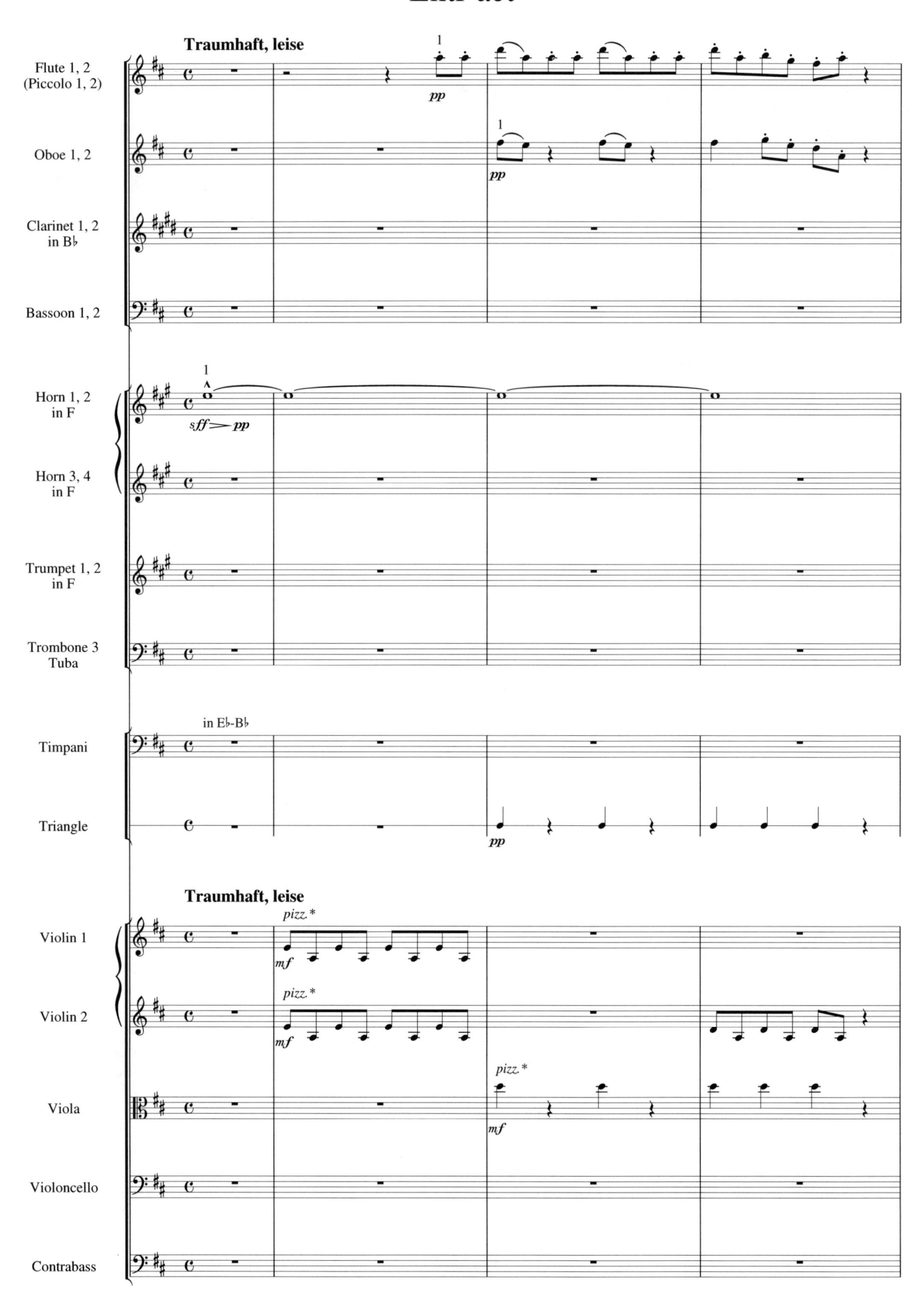

*Alle pizzicati thematisch deutlich.

A
Fl. 1, 2
Ob. 1, 2
Cl. 1, 2
Hn. 1, 2
Tpt. 1, 2
Trgl.
Vn. 1
Vn. 2
Va.
Vc.
Cb.
Vorschläge sehr schnell auszuführen
ppp
pp
sff
[pizz.]
[1]
Bn. 1, 2
poco rit.
morendo
sempre dim. e morendo
sempre dim.
e morendo
dim. e morendo

15
Sehr mässig
Fl. 1, 2
Hn. 1, 2
pppp
verklingend
Vn. 2
Va.
Vc.
Cb.
Dämpfer auf
arco
ppp
divisi
20
Ob. 1, 2
Cl. 1, 2
Bn. 1, 2
pp

B
25
Fl. 1, 2
Ob. 1, 2
Cl. 1, 2
Bn. 1, 2
Hn. 1, 2
Hn. 3, 4
Vn. 1
Vn. 2
Va.
Vc.
Cb.
rit.
[1]
p zart
[1]
pp
pp
con sord.
arco
ppp
rit.

29
Più mosso
Fl. 1, 2
1
p
[1]
Ob. 1, 2
p
Cl. 1, 2
p
Bn. 1, 2
a 2
p
Hn. 1, 2
Hn. 3, 4
Trgl.
p
Più mosso
Vn. 1
senza sord.
pizz.
Vn. 2
senza sord.
pizz.
Va.
senza sord.
pizz.
Vc.
pp
senza sord.
pizz.
Cb.
pp

32
Fl. 1, 2
Ob. 1, 2
Cl. 1, 2
Bn. 1, 2
Hn. 1, 2
Hn. 3, 4
Trgl.
Vn. 1
Vn. 2
Va.
Vc.
Cb.
a 2
1
espress.
pp
poco rit.
ppp
senza sord.
pizz.
poco rit.

*Bemerkung für den Dirigenten: Das *ppp* muss plötzlich und äußerst leise ausgeführt werden.

45
♩. = früher ♩
D
Fl. 1, 2
Ob. 1, 2
Cl. 1, 2
Bn. 1, 2
pp
Hn. 1, 2
Hn. 3, 4
pp
Trgl.
mf
♩. = früher ♩
Vn. 1
senza sord.
pizz.
Vn. 2
senza sord.
pizz.
mf
Va.
senza sord.
pizz.
divisi
mf
Vc.
senza sord.
pizz.
divisi
mf
Cb.
pizz.

50
Fl. 1, 2
Ob. 1, 2
1
pp
Cl. 1, 2
Bn. 1, 2
Hn. 1, 2
1
pp
Hn. 3, 4
3
con sord.
arco
Vn. 1
pp espress.
Vn. 2
Va.
Vc.
con sord.
arco
p espress.
Cb.

215

Sehr breit
cresc.
59
Fl. 1, 2
ppp
a 2
p
pp
Ob. 1, 2
Cl. 1, 2
a 2
Bn. 1, 2
mf
a 2
Hn. 1, 2
mf
Hn. 3, 4
pp
Tpt. 1, 2
Sehr breit
cresc.
Vn. 1
pp molto espress.
Vn. 2
pp molto espress.
arco
Va.
pp espress.
arco
Vc.
pp espress.
divisi
arco
Cb.
pp

63
Wie früher
Fl. 1, 2
Ob. 1, 2
Cl. 1, 2
Bn. 1, 2
Hn. 1, 2
Hn. 3, 4
Tpt. 1, 2
(gestopft)
fpp
fpp
Wie früher
Vn. 1
col legno
p
Vn. 2
col legno
p
Va.
col legno
p
Vc.
pp
Cb.
pp

68
Fl. 1, 2
Ob. 1, 2
Cl. 1, 2
Bn. 1, 2
Hn. 1, 2
Vn. 1
Vn. 2
Va.
Vc.
Cb.
natürlich
pizz.
divisi
natürlich
pizz.
divisi
natürlich
pizz.
pizz.
75
Ob. 1, 2
Cl. 1, 2
Bn. 1, 2
Hn. 1, 2
Vn. 1
Vn. 2
Va.
Vc.
Cb.
sehr schnell
sehr schnell
gestopft
arco

219

Allmählig etwas belebter
Im Anfang sehr mässig wie früher
Hn. 1, 2
Allmählig etwas belebter
Im Anfang sehr mässig wie früher
Vn. 1
Vn. 2
Va.
Vc.
Cb.
senza sord.
arco
pizz.
poco cresc.
Bn. 1, 2
Hn. 1, 2
Hn. 3, 4
Timp.
Vn. 1
Vn. 2
Va.
Vc.
Cb.
[offen]
divisi
arco
pp espress.
poco cresc.

104
Nicht schnell
Fl. 1, 2
pp
poco cresc.
Ob. 1, 2
pp
poco cresc.
Cl. 1, 2
1
pp espress.
poco cresc.
Bn. 1, 2
fpp
pp
poco cresc.
Hn. 1, 2
a 2
pp
sehr zart
[1]
pp
poco cresc.
Hn. 3, 4
pp
sehr zart
Tpt. 1, 2
Nicht schnell
Vn. 1
fpp
Vn. 2
pp espress.
poco cresc.
Va.
sehr zart
pp espress.
poco cresc.
Vc.
sehr zart
pizz.
Cb.
pp
pizz.

108
poco rit.
Fl. 1, 2
Ob. 1, 2
1
Cl. 1, 2
Bn. 1, 2
[1]
Hn. 1, 2
Hn. 3, 4
Tpt. 1, 2
poco rit.
Vn. 1
pizz.
Vn. 2
pizz.
Va.
Vc.
Cb.

112
E
Sehr zart, a tempo moderato
Fl. 1, 2
Ob. 1, 2
1
p espress.
Cl. 1, 2
1
p
Bn. 1, 2
Hn. 1, 2
1
pp
espress.
Hn. 3, 4
Tpt. 1, 2
Sehr zart, a tempo moderato
divisi
Springbogen
Vn. 1
[arco]
Vn. 2
[arco]
Va.
p
Vc.
Cb.

224

F
122
Fl. 1, 2
Ob. 1, 2
Cl. 1, 2
[1]
p espress.
p
Bn. 1, 2
p
1
pp
Hn. 1, 2
p
Hn. 3, 4
3
pp
Tpt. 1, 2
Vn. 1
pp
Vn. 2
pp
Va.
p
Vc.
p
espress.
Cb.

127
Fl. 1, 2
Ob. 1, 2
Cl. 1, 2
Bn. 1, 2
Hn. 1, 2
Hn. 3, 4
Tpt. 1, 2
Vn. 1
Vn. 2
Va.
Vc.
Cb.
1
3
p
pizz.

131
Fl. 1, 2
a 2
mf
Ob. 1, 2
[1]
p
Cl. 1, 2
p
Bn. 1, 2
1
Hn. 1, 2
pp
Hn. 3, 4
pp
Tpt. 1, 2
Vn. 1
Vn. 2
tr
Va.
[divisi]
p espress.
Vc.
[divisi]
arco
p [espress.]
Cb.

135
Immer noch sehr zart
Fl. 1, 2
p
poco cresc.
Ob. 1, 2
p
poco cresc.
Cl. 1, 2
1
p
poco cresc.
Bn. 1, 2
1
p
poco cresc.
Hn. 1, 2
[1]
p
poco cresc.
Hn. 3, 4
Tpt. 1, 2
Immer noch sehr zart
Vn. 1
poco cresc.
Vn. 2
p
poco cresc.
Va.
p
[poco cresc.]
Vc.
pizz.
Cb.

229

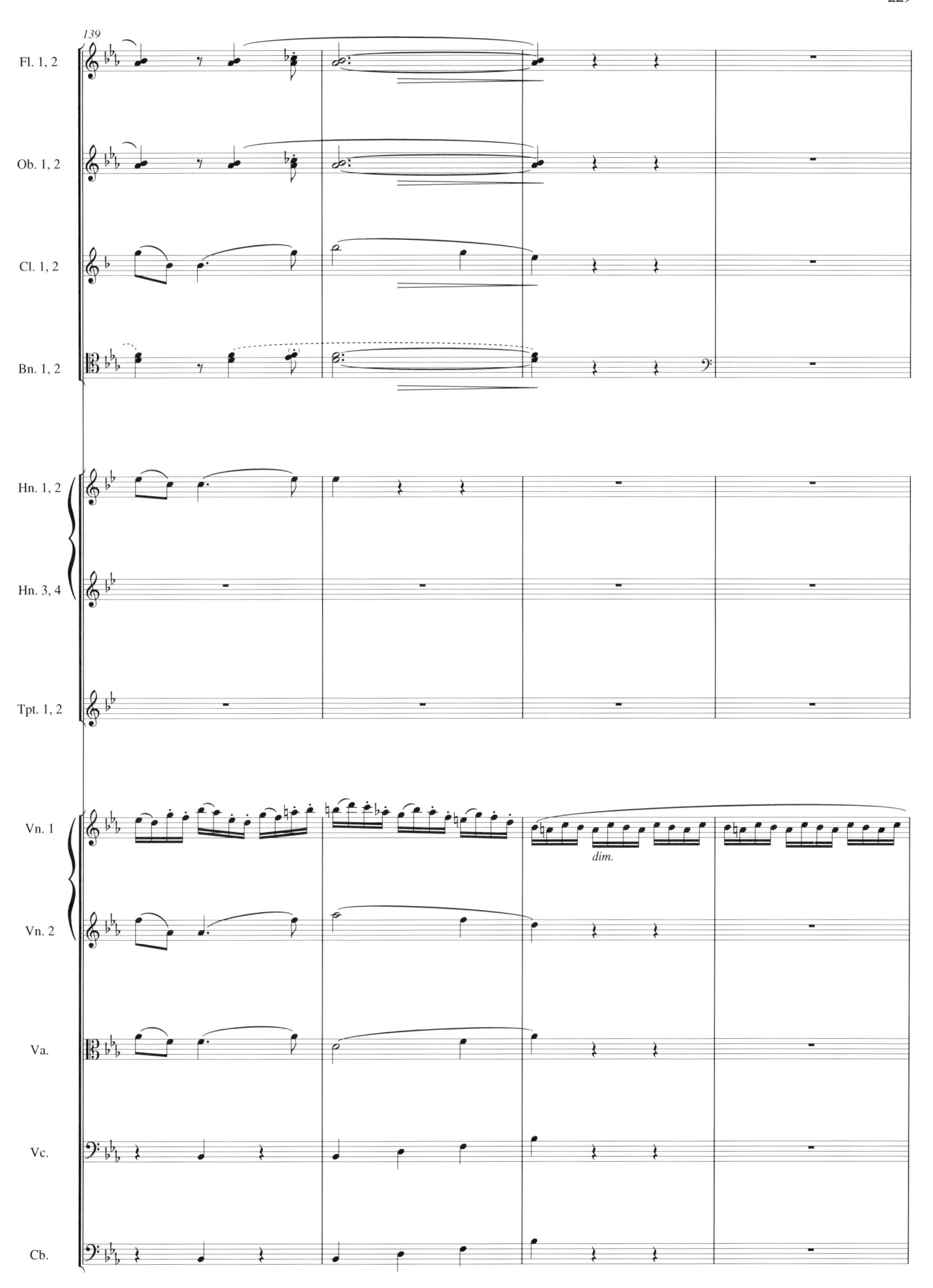

G
Breit und schwungvoll
(Von hier an erst im Tempo und dynamisch steigern)
143
Fl. 1, 2
Ob. 1, 2
Cl. 1, 2
Bn. 1, 2
[a 2]
a 2
Hn. 1, 2
Hn. 3, 4
Tpt. 1, 2
Breit und schwungvoll
(Von hier an erst im Tempo und dynamisch steigern)
Vn. 1
Vn. 2
Va.
Vc.
Cb.
pizz.
arco
molto espress.

148
Fl. 1, 2
a 2
p
Ob. 1, 2
a 2
Cl. 1, 2
a 2
Bn. 1, 2
Hn. 1, 2
p
a 2
a 2
Hn. 3, 4
a 2
Tpt. 1, 2
Vn. 1
Vn. 2
Va.
Vc.
Cb.

152
Fl. 1, 2
a 2
cresc.
Ob. 1, 2
a 2
cresc.
Cl. 1, 2
a 2
cresc.
Bn. 1, 2
a 2
cresc.
Hn. 1, 2
a 2
[cresc.]
Hn. 3, 4
a 2
a 2
cresc.
Tpt. 1, 2
Vn. 1
cresc.
Vn. 2
cresc.
Va.
cresc.
Vc.
[cresc.]
Cb.
arco
pizz.

233

161
a 2
poco rit.
Fl. 1, 2
ff
Ob. 1, 2
Cl. 1, 2
Bn. 1, 2
Hn. 1, 2
f
Hn. 3, 4
Tpt. 1, 2
1
mf
Timp.
Vn. 1
Vn. 2
Va.
Vc.
Cb.

J
Wiedersehr breit
Più mosso
165
Fl. 1, 2
Ob. 1, 2
Cl. 1, 2
Bn. 1, 2
Hn. 1, 2
Hn. 3, 4
a 2
Tpt. 1, 2
Trb. 3
Tb.
mf
Timp.
f
Wieder sehr breit
Più mosso
Vn. 1
Vn. 2
Va.
Vc.
Cb.

molto rit.
170
a 2
Fl. 1, 2
Ob. 1, 2
Cl. 1, 2
Bn. 1, 2
Hn. 1, 2
Hn. 3, 4
[a 2]
Tpt. 1, 2
f
Trb. 3
Tb.
Timp.
tr
Vn. 1
Vn. 2
Va.
Vc.
Cb.

Recent Researches in the Music of the Nineteenth and Early Twentieth Centuries
Rufus Hallmark, general editor

Vol.	Composer: *Title*
1–2	Jan Ladislav Dussek: *Selected Piano Works*
3–4	Johann Nepomuk Hummel: *Piano Concerto, Opus 113*
5	*One Hundred Years of Eichendorff Songs*
6	Etienne-Nicolas Méhul: *Symphony No. 1 in G Minor*
7–8	*Embellished Opera Arias*
9	*The Nineteenth-Century Piano Ballade: An Anthology*
10	*Famous Poets, Neglected Composers: Songs to Lyrics by Goethe, Heine, Mörike, and Others*
11	Charles-Marie Widor: *The Symphonies for Organ: Symphonie I*
12	Charles-Marie Widor: *The Symphonies for Organ: Symphonie II*
13	Charles-Marie Widor: *The Symphonies for Organ: Symphonie III*
14	Charles-Marie Widor: *The Symphonies for Organ: Symphonie IV*
15	Charles-Marie Widor: *The Symphonies for Organ: Symphonie V*
16	Charles-Marie Widor: *The Symphonies for Organ: Symphonie VI*
17	Charles-Marie Widor: *The Symphonies for Organ: Symphonie VII*
18	Charles-Marie Widor: *The Symphonies for Organ: Symphonie VIII*
19	Charles-Marie Widor: *The Symphonies for Organ: Symphonie gothique*
20	Charles-Marie Widor: *The Symphonies for Organ: Symphonie romane*
21	Archduke Rudolph of Austria: *Forty Variations on a Theme by Beethoven for Piano; Sonata in F Minor for Violin and Piano*
22	Fanny Hensel: *Songs for Pianoforte, 1836–1837*
23	*Anthology of Goethe Songs*
24	Walter Rabl: *Complete Instrumental Chamber Works*
25	Stefano Pavesi: *Dies irae concertato*
26	Franz Liszt: *St. Stanislaus: Scene 1, Two Polonaises, Scene 4*
27	George Frederick Pinto: *Three Sonatas for Pianoforte with Violin*
28	Felix Mendelssohn: *Concerto for Two Pianos and Orchestra in E Major (1823): Original Version of the First Movement*
29	Johann Nepomuk Hummel: *Mozart's* Haffner *and* Linz *Symphonies*
30–31	Gustav Mahler: *Die drei Pintos: Based on Sketches and Original Music of Carl Maria von Weber*